THE WAR IS NOT OVER

by

JANA STAMPS

&

BILL STAMPS

Copyright © 2021 Bill & Jana Stamps

All rights reserved.

To the best of my memory, all events, locales and conversations are true. Some names have been changed to protect the privacy of a handful of individuals.

Once again, I would like to thank Dr. C. K. Phillips for his very kind assistance with helping complete this book. Be sure to check out his books @ https://www.amazon.com/gp/product/B074BDDD6V

TABLE OF CONTENTS

TABLE OF CONTENTS...5

BILL STAMPS..9

FOREWARD...13

THE LAST HOUR: 17

CHAPTER I...20

DEDICATION, Randy Fox..21

   THE STORY BEHIND THE STORY "THANK YOU, JESUS, FOR COLD WATER"..29

   THANK YOU, JESUS, FOR COLD WATER 45

HAPPY BIRTHDAY MARINES: 244 CANDLES......60

TO ALL MY FELLOW VETERANS..........74

BELATED HAPPY BIRTHDAY TO THE MARINES AND HAPPY VETERAN'S DAY TO US ALL..........76

DUFFY..........89

REMEMBERING ALL OUR HEROES THIS MEMORIAL DAY..........107

ENDURING THOUGHTS AT 3 AM 120

CHAPTER II..........127

BILL'S LAST STORIES AND PERSONAL COMMENTARY. 129

IN MEMORY OF BILL STAMPS, By William Wright..........134

IN RECOGNITION OF MY BEST FRIEND..........................139

DEAR GOD, THANK YOU FOR CREATING WATER..........152

A WHOLE NEW DECADE TO GET IT RIGHT 166

THESE LAST FEW YEARS HAVE BEEN A TRIP..................180

OLD BARNS AND SOUTHERN MEMORIES.......................194

IT'S, REALLY, ALL ABOUT THE TRUTH............................209

WHEN DID IT ALL BECOME SO POLITICAL?...................220

THIS YEAR, 2020, CAN KISS IT WHERE THE SUN DON'T SHINE..231

HOLLYWOOD DRINKIN' DAYS AND LASH LARUE..........241

THE LAST NIGHT...253

ADDENDUM:..256

BILL'S LAST STORY..258

THINKING ABOUT LIVING SOME MORE........................260

FEELS LIKE..269

GOOD GRIEF, By Wanda Mayfield.....................................270

FINAL THOUGHTS...272

THANK YOU to Dr. CK Phillips..287

CONTACT INFO...289

Bill Stamps

October 2, 1948 – March 10, 2021

It's all about the dash, really. That small line between two dates of a person's life. This is not an original thought of mine. I heard it somewhere, a long time ago.

I am grief-stricken beyond words by the loss of my beloved. A power-house man with a heart of gold. He no longer has to shoulder the burden of the cross he carried all his life. He is now free to soar. His body was getting weary, but his spirit is alive.

The last earthly words I heard him speak were for the Almighty to forgive him. I will love you forever and mourn your suffering.

Many have gotten to know Bill through his weekly newspaper columns. First in the Cleveland Daily Banner then onto the Chattanooga Times Free Press. His uncanny ability to transcend space and time to go fetch nuggets of stories from a bygone era is second to none. He was so modest about his writing, choosing instead to see himself as the vessel for a God-given talent. At least that's what I told him.

I have always been very proud of his combat service with the Marine Corps., at the height of the war in Vietnam. Bill was an S-2 Scout, point-man, Delta 1/3. He was awarded three Purple Hearts, the Bronze Star, the Silver Star and the Vietnamese Cross of Gallantry (Combat V), while serving under the command of Medal of Honor recipient, Colonel Wesley L. Fox.

In parting, and in Bill's memory, I humbly request for you to please spread, far and wide, the word of

Bill's two other written creations: MIZ LENA and SOUTHERN FOLKS .

It's Vintage. Americana.

On behalf of Bill, thank you for everything. He left us with these last words, "A lot of sweet people out there. Stay well and thanks for being my friends."

God bless you.

~Jana

FOREWARD

March 9 – March 10, 2021
11 p.m. – 2 a.m.

Don't let anybody fool you into thinking that a heart attack will kill you on the spot. It took 3 hours for Bill to pass. His inner strength was doing all it could to keep living. According to the doctor and nurse, he was trying to sit up while they were working on his heart.

Prior to the paramedics showing up, Bill told me he was going into shock. He started having a seizure, then another. Foaming at the mouth and clenching his jaw so tightly that he was suffocating. I had to pry his mouth open and go fetch his tongue for him to breathe. It was violent and atrocious to witness.

I've previously stated that the last earthly words I heard Bill speak were for the Lord to forgive him. In the ambulance, while continuing to have a heart attack, I heard him yell "Incoming." My shattered heart broke into a million bits at the sound of him back on the battlefield in Vietnam.

Once they got him to the hospital, I was imploring them to do something to stop his pain. I heard a nurse say "I gave him morphine." That didn't seem to be alleviating the obvious struggle he was in.

After that, it was us running down hallways, up an elevator, down another hallway to the door of the operating room.

I was led to a waiting room. No one in sight for what seemed like an eternity. It was stark and quiet like a tomb. Time and space stopped. Suddenly, here they come. "We're working on him, but it doesn't look good." Gut-punch shock and devastation. Another hour, then the grim return of the masked doctors in the middle of the night.

They led me in to see him and warned me of blood and tubes. He was covered in a sheet, his face showing. He was cold. Life was slipping away. I caressed his head and kissed his cheek and whispered over my tears "I love you, my sweet angel, you are my most precious baby. I'm so sorry. I will love you forever." His eyes were closed but I saw a sliver of his one eye as I looked at him for the last time.

THE LAST HOUR

March 13, 2021

Bill's son, Jesse, and I released our most precious father and husband to the arms of our Creator, yesterday.

There were 12 of us in attendance.

Milteen Cartwright and I administered anointment of Bill's body and soul, in his last hour.

We were blessed to be surrounded by close friends and immediate family.

And, a room full of "Amazing Grace." I felt in the presence of Spirit.

Bill had a big heart and an even bigger soul. He was also known to be brutally honest. There never was a doubt as to where he stood on things. We were together for 26 years and hardly ever spent a day apart.

One sentence that keeps running in my mind is:

"He had to die for us to live."

There are only two of us who know the magnitude of what that really means.

Bill left it all on the table. The ultimate sacrifice. The depth of this emotion is nearly unbearable.

My love for you is eternal.

I have found my real family through the blood of Jesus Christ our Savior.

May my baby, finally, rest in peace.

Amen

CHAPTER I

DEDICATION

Randy Fox

It's with great honor and pleasure that we dedicate this book to our great friend, Randy Fox. Bill would have wanted it this way.

Randy's a man like no other around. He's special. A little gruff on the outside, but an angel inside. He is fiercely loyal to his sweetheart wife, Betty, of 49 years; to his friends; his family, daughter Sandy; son, David; granddaughter Nola and grandson Ben. God. Country. And, Elvis.

Back in 2015, Randy convinced Bill to get on Facebook. All their friends from school were on it. Bill had been so isolated, I felt it would do him some good to regain a sense of connection to the world. That's when he started writing. He always said that living in Cleveland, Tennessee "were the best three years of my childhood." A place where people still know what it means to live their faith. No frills necessary to the truth. It's simple that way.

Randy was drafted to go to Vietnam (January 69-70). Army Grunt. 4th Battalion, 21st Infantry, 11th Brigade, Americal Division.

He, too, endured the drudgery of that horrible war. We've heard people refer to the war in Vietnam as a "conflict." Such a slap in the face of these men who lived through Hell, daily, for unending months. Sometimes, years.

Randy is a good man. Like Bill, the thought of killing goes against the very fiber of their being. It's not in their nature. They sacrificed the purity of their soul doing what was right for their country. At least that's what they were led to believe. A whole generation comprised of some of the most devoted, talented and good-natured boys were sent to slaughter. Then the return. Can you imagine that happening to you? What incredible hurt and disrespect. How dare anyone judge them upon their return? Spit on them. Expect them to return to "normal."

Bill and Randy would have late night private message "talks." Try to cheer each other up. Sometimes a little morbidly. It took Bill a long long time to finally realize he was suffering from PTSD, also. Agent Orange and its non-disclosed symptoms. Shattered nervous system. For all those years of repressed injuries, feelings and overall neglect, Bill faced the boomerang effect. All at once. He once wrote "I hope to go out with my boots on and a twinkle in my eyes." His boots were on. The twinkle I saw when I last kissed him was just a slither of his eye telling me he loved me.

Randy has been like a brother to me, too. He's tended to my heart and let me cry while I talk about Bill. That's the most precious gift someone can give you, while grieving so deeply.

Randy, you are a sweet special man. Bill and I love you. Your many friends and family in Cleveland and Bradley County love you, too. You have served your country and your community honorably and with the highest standards of dignity. You have done so in a quiet, selfless manner.

Aside from faithfully delivering the mail to countless families around Bradley County, Randy worked as a detective in the 70's with his great pal, the late and one-and-only Charlie McKenzie, Bradley County Deputy Sheriff. There are some funny stories of those two. Furthermore, Randy has served on countless boards with his good friend, the late, great, Jerry Frazier.

But, one of Randy's greatest accomplishments in the civilian world was to instigate, 36 years ago, The South East Tennessee Community Corrections. An alternative sentencing program that gives first-time offenders a second chance at redemption. The program has since been adopted state-wide and continues to be very successful.

Randy's the best of the best. He's true grit Tennessee.

God bless you always. ~Jana

Bill and his sister, Heather

THE STORY BEHIND THE STORY
THANK YOU, JESUS, FOR COLD WATER

Thank You, Jesus, for Cold Water is the first of a handful of stories Bill wrote about Vietnam, over the course of his five years, publishing weekly, first for the *Cleveland Daily Banner*, then to *Chattanooga Times Free Press*.

I'm not exactly sure what prompted Bill to write this story, but it's very special to me. It took so much out of him. We were both crushed with emotion after reading the final draft.

Somehow, ironically, it seemed to have a cathartic effect as well. As though it was meant to be written. A higher force of destiny. Plus, Bill's ability to write so naturally paints such a poignant portrait of human suffering. It's not a documentary, a movie or some historical account. These are stories about real people. Young men, with blood running through their veins, just like you and me.

"If he could just find his people again, they would understand him."

Those were my ongoing thoughts, along with constant nightly prayers, knees to the ground. We were so lost and alone in a world that had no time for the broken and memories of a war long forgotten. The little glimmer of Light that was still burning in us was teeter-tottering on extinction.

The story of a slow descent, begins, of course, years prior.

Bill never got treated for the many ailments he suffered not only physically, mentally, but emotionally, when he came back from Vietnam.

In his younger years, and because of his tremendous constitution, he muscled his way through the constant pains and demons that ran through his mind and body, along with many pieces of shrapnel that would occasionally come to the surface of the skin and need extraction. His ankle, back, head and knee took the worst of it. Add Agent Orange which was dumped on these poor souls, and malaria brought on by mosquitoes the size of humming birds. Not just malaria, but falciparum malaria. The most fatal kind.

Christmas season, 2015 was far from joyous for us. All the repressed anger and hurt that had been bottled up since childhood and made worse by family deception, came raging through Bill's body and consumed his mind. We had seemingly lost it all. There did not appear to be any bright tomorrows left for us.

That's when I called the suicide line at the VA. Nice people, but of no substantial help. I understand things have changed since, for the better. I couldn't afford to let them cart him away by the cops and put him in a hospital. Locking him up somewhere would have killed him. Bill was acutely claustrophobic. All I could do was love him. Stay close to him. He pleaded for me to leave him. Telling me I was still young and could start over. How could I ever do that to him? He who had given so much of himself to me, his country, his family and friends. And, a parade of random people in need of a step up.

At that same time, Bill wandered off. When I went to fetch him, I saw him staggering down the road, like one of those homeless people talking to themselves. I understand all too well how some lose their minds. Bill did, that day. It's a hopeless feeling to witness your loved one in such despair. All I could do was pray.

Some have heard Bill say that I saved him. The truth is, years prior, he's the one who saved me. His insistence on brutal truth. No pirouetting around facts. A hard line that led me to Redemption. He's the one who gave me a chance at happiness with a fiercely loyal man. One who would give his life for me and, ultimately, I believe, did just so. We were both dying. Our feet were stuck in mud. There wasn't enough oxygen for the two of us to keep living.

It had taken him many years into our relationship before he opened up about having served in combat in the Marine Corps., in Vietnam. I could tell it was a sensitive subject, so I let him talk when he wanted to and started asking questions as discreetly as possible. Concerned about jarring too many brutal visuals. In retrospect, I probably was afraid of grasping the full scope of the atrociousness of that war and measure of the inhumane suffering. Things I could never unhear. Though he spared me all things too gory, always, I could see him reliving, in an endless loop, moments no human being should witness, ever.

Little did I realize that not only had he served, but he was an S-2 Scout. Being point-man, means you're the first guy up front of the platoon, the scout. He was escorted by 3 Vietnamese soldiers who had been rehabilitated. That's the most polite way I can describe their service.

So, here we are a few days before Christmas 2015, in a hotel room, waiting for Divine Intervention.

Two weeks prior, we'd been jolted when we got word our most precious pup, Scout, had died in the kennel where we had to leave our pups. Turned out it wasn't Scout, but Chief, our youngest, who had died. As heart-broken as we were about Chief, we felt like God had given us a sign. Another chance. Scout, Bill's most precious pup, was resurrected from the dead! When I told Bill about the miraculous turn of events, that morning when he got up, I thought he was going to have a heart-attack. He started hyper-ventilating. A few minutes prior to that, he told me, he was in the bathroom telling God he didn't think he could make it another day.

It's my opinion that every combat vet should have a dog. It's the greatest therapy there is.

Flashback to 2010, Scout was the one who had gone to fetch the last glimmer of hope still alive in Bill, then.

To know Scout was a blessing. With age, he became as sweet as a lamb. As a child-doggie he was on the wild side. We weren't quite convinced he was a dog for the first several years of his life. He was more like a gremlin.

That day in May, 2010, Scout was racing around the corner of the house and saw Bill sitting on the patio sobbing. As uncivilized as was Scout, he stopped on a dime and went and lay on Bill's feet. I know he saved my baby's heart that day. Bill had been betrayed by the closest person to his heart. His Achille's heal. That's when I recognized in him the wounded warrior he was. Life as I knew it, vanished.

Beware of the Judas in your life. This is not a metaphor. We all continue to play a part in the big picture.

It's only then that I saw the magnitude of Bill's broken heart and found myself transmuted to the battlefield with him. Glacial. He had been mortally wounded and left to die. That's when my next level of devotion to him really began. He wasn't just my beloved, he was also a warrior who needed help. Deserved the dignity of being recognized for the immeasurable sacrifice he'd given of himself. I couldn't let him die by himself of his wounds. From then on, I took care of him, as best I could shoulder, by myself.

Bill didn't die that day. It took 10 years for him to expire from that fatal blow to the heart.

Being broke is the inability to pay your bills. Poverty is when you worry about your next meal and that of your pets.

Some have wondered, and others have gossiped, about why I didn't "just go get a job." Bill was my job. My responsibility. I couldn't ever leave him alone. I represented the only security he had. He would worry about my safety, constantly. As did I, about his.

They used to call it "shell shocked."

PTSD gets thrown around so much these days that the meaning of the word itself has been diluted. One should never confuse PTSD from the battlefield with any other trauma. It's different.

Imagine having the worst nightmare and it never going away. Even when awake. Visions of Marines laying in ditches, bloated from the heat. The smell of death everywhere. Bodies with their manly parts cut off, stuck in their mouths and sawn up. Terror.

Or, the walking dead. The Marine staggering towards them as they tell him to hit the ground, only to have him walk past them and collapse. His entire back blown out. These are only a few of the stories Bill could tell. He went native.

He never could forgive himself for the things he did over there. I would tell him he had to, in order to survive. That never alleviated the terrible guilt and shame he carried all his life. He was such a pure soul.

When Bill wrote *Thank you Jesus for Cold Water* days before that 2015 Christmas, and posted it on Facebook, our hearts felt like we had given this world all that was left of us. I prayed for the Lord to take us.

Just as all hope seemed to have vanished, our good friend, Randy Fox, an Army Vietnam combat vet and to whom this book is dedicated, wrote "A+." I burst into tears. There still was someone out there who cared and remembered.

Shortly thereafter, we settle in Cleveland, Tennessee, *The City with Spirit*. A place full of loving, kind people who embraced us as their own and nurtured our soul back from the brink.

Bill's many readers encouraged him, week after week, to keep writing his stories and always expressed deep empathy and appreciation for the cerebral journey.

Some of Bill's most poignant stories were those he wrote about his time overseas. They all got published on special occasion, in recognition of the sacrifice of those who serve(d) in combat: Independance Day, Marine Corps. Birthday, Veteran's Day and Memorial Day. Like a window in time allowing the reader a digestible glimpse into that gory tragedy and the unnecessary slaughter of so many.

I believe God, the people of Cleveland and surrounding area, gave Bill the stamina to live the extra 5 years needed for him to write over 120 short stories.

Thank You, Jesus, for Cold Water is the first of them.

These men who gave it all should not be forgotten.

War is a business.

As long as a lonely few make fortunes off of it, men, women, children and generations of families will have to suffer the collateral damage.

Wives are the forgotten ones who land on the front-line of the war back home.

It is through faith alone that we walked together through *The Valley of the Shadow of Death.* ~Jana

THANK YOU, JESUS, FOR COLD WATER

As I continue to walk down life's road, I find myself thinking back. Not ahead. It's not digression. There's plenty to keep me in the present. I guess, I just haven't had or taken the time, up until now, to sit still and think about something other than making my next deal. They say that once you've reached a certain age and not consumed with work, you start thinking about things that you've stuffed away. That's me.

I spent four years in the Marine Corps and did my time in Viet Nam. I, like many, maybe even most, of my fellow combat veterans, suffer from PTSD. I'm not nearly as bad off as a lot of them, but I have my moments. Before I left for Nam, anyone who knew me back then, will tell you that I was the life of the party. When I came back from my overseas tour, I was a changed man. Things that used to matter, didn't anymore and vice versa.

I've had problems sleeping for years. All through my 20's and 30's, as soon as I drifted off, I was back in the jungle. I took drugs and drank myself under the tables of some of the finest watering holes in Los

Angeles. They tell me that I had a good time. Anything, to take my mind off of all the junk.

Even though my profession as a promoter pretty much dictated that I be the center of attention, I couldn't wait to get home and away from the crowds. Too much time in a crowded store or getting bumped, walking down the sidewalk, makes we want to break away. Five hours in an airplane is the most that I can go.

I hate hunting. Frankly, it feels more like ambushing to me. I've killed enough. As was told to me, many years ago, once you've taken another man's life, you'll never be the same. It's true. It's one of those things you try not to think about. You file it somewhere and say a prayer, before you go to bed, that it won't come back to you in your dreams. It works, most of the time.

I tend to stay away from loud noises. And loud people, for that matter. Redneck-mufflers, sirens, bangs and booms, and loudness, in general, bugs me. When I first got back from overseas, to "the world", as we used to call it, there was more than one time I hit the ground as a result of an unexpected loud noise. Combat reflexes. It was embarrassing.

It took years of therapy for me to be able to have a disagreement with someone without smacking them. I'm really sorry about those times. I hurt some people. I could go from calm to a storm in a matter of seconds. It's taken me a long time to learn how to control my temper. I can't really blame it all on Viet Nam. I've always had a temper. Booze never helped matters.

After you've survived life-or-death situations, almost everything else seems trivial. You get a big dose of reality and your priorities realign. Spending too much time on stuff that really doesn't matter that much is agonizing to me. I keep the dander down by doing my best to stay away from arguments and stupidity.

All this stated, as I've gotten older, I've become much more tolerant and compassionate. No more knee-jerk reactions. I have to give credit to my wife,

Jana, for that. When you love someone, with all your heart, they make you want to be a better person. It's hard to explain, but love, real love, is a first-class remedy for almost anything.

Way-back years ago, my grandmother, Miz Lena, told me, "No matter what's goin' on, always remember to thank Jesus for every day of yore life. Never ask Him for more than yuh need. Just simple pleasures. Always keep yore promises that yuh make to the Lord, and He'll keep lookin' out for yuh."

So, for the better part of my life, I've done just that. I try not to ask God for much other than what I need. I must confess, I've made a few promises to the Almighty that I didn't keep. Many of them in an inebriated state of being. More than a few times, I've blurted out, "Please, God, if you'll just stop this room from spinning, I'll never drink again." Maybe a little late on my promises, but I finally stopped drinking ten years ago.

I have to believe that the Lord is indeed forgiving, because, for the most part, up through now, I've had a pretty good life.

I go out of my way to treat those less fortunate than I with respect, understanding, courtesy and empathy. That's just the way we "Children of the South" were raised. Most always, if I see a veteran in a bad way, I'm happy to monetarily contribute to his need. So many of those brave men I fought alongside, in the jungles and rice paddies of Vietnam, have not been able to rid their minds of the gore and devastation of that tragic time. They just can't shake it.

One thing's for certain. Every one of us got much closer to God. I've never done so much praying in my life. It was the same prayer over-and-over, "Please, God, don't let me die over here." We all said the same prayer, continuously. Some of us made it. Many were called Home to the Lord, early. Their young departures from this world caused so many American families gut-wrenching anguish. They were to never be the same, again.

The same families that proudly flew our flag in their yards and rubbed decals onto their car bumpers and back windows stating that their son was in the Armed Forces. The prayers they launched, asking the Heavens to watch over their boy and safely deliver him back home to them. Parents and wives, dreading a knock on the front door, in the middle of the night, and opening it to two men in military uniforms with a piece of paper in their hands, locked jaws and a sad, grim look on their faces.

There were buckets of tears shed on those porches. Women sobbing. Their heads buried into the valor-decorated chests of those men who came bearing the bad news. Before they left, they presented the family with a perfectly folded American flag and were told that their son or husband died as a grown-up man, defending our country's freedom and way of life. If nothing else, they could hold on to that. That he had been brave and died a great American.

It was a nasty, sweaty 120 degrees. I was lying in a rice paddy, just beyond the village of Dai Do. I was hit. I lay on my back, with my left knee ripped open from enemy shrapnel. I made a tourniquet out of a torn drab-green t-shirt and waited my turn to be choppered back to the rear.

All around me were dead and wounded Marines. Almost all of them were praying out loud. Screaming into the air, already full with the explosions of war, begging to God. It's hard to describe the desperate, gurgling pleas of dying men calling out for their mothers. It's even harder to drown those sounds from my head.

I prayed, too. I was pretty sure that I wasn't going to die from my wound. Still, I prayed. It was hot as Hell. Death smells. Once you've smelled it, you never forget it. It stays with you for life. It can make you sick to your stomach.

Crazy thoughts run through your head when you're challenging death and defying the odds. Of all things, surrounded by death and chaos, I started thinking about what Grand Mom told me about thanking God for every day of my life. To ask for simple pleasures.

So, right then and there, I thanked Jesus for that day of my life and asked for a simple pleasure. Cold water. You never get cold water out in the "bush." I promised the Almighty that if He answered my prayer, that I would never again take cold water for granted.

I lost some blood. I'd pass out, then come back to, then, pass out, again. I woke up in a make-shift hospital in Quang Tri.

My knee had been stitched up and wrapped. I looked up and saw a nurse standing over me and smiling down at me. I was woozy from morphine. At first, I thought she was an angel. She said, "Hello, Sweetie. You're alive and your knee will be just fine." Then she asked, "Would you like a glass of cold water?"

Miz Lena also used to tell me, "The Lord works in mysterious ways." Beyond a shadow of doubt, that was the best tasting cold water I've ever had. To this day, every time I have a drink of cold water, I say out loud or think, "Thank you, Jesus, for cold water."

Today's a special one for countless American families. A day of reflection. The one day of the year that commemorates and celebrates our country's heroes and warriors of foreign wars. A bunch of young men, from all walks of life, who gave it their all and survived or went down swinging.

I can only speak for myself. But, I know there are a lot of good men out there who made it back but not without scars. Physical and mental scars. For some, the war's not over. It's still in their heads. I believe God has a special place in his heart for these veterans. I hope so.

So, send a little prayer up to Heaven and thank the Almighty that you're an American and give thanks for those boys who made sacrifices for their homeland. For their beloved America.

While you're at it, ask God to watch over our brave servicemen and women, who are out there somewhere, protecting our freedom and are continuously praying the same prayer to God as did we.

HAPPY BIRTHDAY MARINES:
244 CANDLES

I really couldn't blame Dad for not wanting me to hang around town. I'd been a handful to deal with all through my high school years. If they'd had a trophy for the kid who got into the most trouble, I'd have won by a landslide.

When they told me, after my one and only semester of college, that I hadn't made the cut, I packed up and came home. I guess I should have taken education more seriously. Vietnam was revving up.

The next thing I knew, I was meeting the Marine Corps recruiter in Dad's office at the radio station. I signed up for four years. They gave me 90 days to get my affairs squared away.

Right after the first of the year, they mailed me a package. Inside was a government-issued one-way Greyhound bus ticket and orders to report to the Marine Corps Recruit Depot, San Diego, March, 1967.

There wasn't much for me to do. When you get on that bus, all you need are the clothes on your back and a few bucks in your pocket. Everything in your future is provided to you by Uncle Sam, right down to your skivvies and a toothbrush.

I used my 90 days wisely. I took out as many girls as I could. Hands down, telling a girl that, "I hope I make it back" is the very best bachelor line I've ever spoken. Those were three of the best months of my life.

Early, that rainy March morning, Dad drove me to the bus depot. We had a few minutes before boarding. I don't remember what we talked about. It was awkward chit-chat. I wondered if it crossed Dad's mind that I might be heading off to war and never come back.

In the late 1950s, after he got off the air, Dad drove over to Franklin, Tennessee and brought my two younger brothers and I back to Cleveland to live with him. Mom had some serious personal problems. She just wasn't capable of taking care of us any longer.

With the exception of two short summer visits and an hour on a Christmas morning, we hadn't had much contact with Dad in the past few years. It was quite apparent that Dad had been living a much better life than Mom and us boys.

When kids are put in the middle of their parents' differences, unfortunately, sides get chosen. At the time, I favored my mother, but I recognized that Dad provided stability and security that Mom never could.

Through the years, Dad and I developed a deep and loving relationship. As a matter of fact, I loved him very much. Still, I couldn't help myself from having mixed feelings about the way he had treated Mom. I guess it showed.

Also, it hurt that Dad was rather reserved with his heart, when it came to me. Things got better between us in the final ten years of his life.

Just before I got on the bus, uncharacteristically, Dad gave me a tight hug and kissed the side of my face. He had tears and a little tremble in his voice.

He told me, "You're leaving as a boy, and you'll come back a man. Be the best Marine you can be." I thought about that all the way down to San Diego. I decided that was exactly what I was going to do.

Boot Camp was as tough as I'd heard it was. They tear you down and build you back up in three-and-a-half months. They toughen you up physically and mentally. Two days before graduation, the Platoon Commander had us fall-in outside our Quonset huts and read off our MOSs (military occupational specialty) and where we were heading.

Most of the guys were ordered to report to Staging for more combat training, then saddle up and board a flight to Vietnam. Their MOS was 0311.

Ground Forces. Grunts. The heart and soul of the "lean-green-fighting-machine." God has a special place in his heart for grunts.

Out of the entire Battalion, I was the only one given an 0231 MOS. Intelligence. I had no idea what I'd be doing. My orders read for me to report to the Commanding Officer of the Fifth Engineers Battalion, Fifth Marine Division, Camp Pendleton, California.

From there, I was sent to Vietnamese Language School and then intense training at Guerilla Warfare School. After all that training, I was assigned a desk and a typewriter. I was an "office pinkie", typing Secret Clearances and reduced to complete embarrassment.

I kept requesting that I be sent to Vietnam. I hadn't joined the Marines to sit behind a desk. Finally, almost a year later, I received my orders to report to Staging.

We were less than a week away from shoving off for Nam, when I got the word that my brother, Ricky, had fallen off a cliff and into the river. Three weeks after we buried him, I was in-country. I took Ricky's spirit with me.

We flew into Da Nang. The Viet Cong were dropping mortars on the airstrip as we landed. My heart was racing. I told myself to just cool it. I drew strength by remembering lines from Rudyard Kipling's letter to his son. A poem entitled, "If." Most especially, the line about keeping your head about you, while the rest of them are losing theirs.

I'd never seen anything like it. Structures and helicopters on fire, and the first of many dead Marines I would see. Bodies strewn out and lying on the runway. Their stillness was eerie. It was like the Almighty had turned off the sound and created a small capsule of stand-still time for my fellow Marines' souls to ascend to the sky and beyond.

Patriotic families would soon hear the news of their sons' death and, through their tears, look up to God and scream at Him, "Why ?"

Like magic, between my extensive combat training, Ricky in my heart, and Dad's ringing words to me about being a good Marine, I became calm and focused.

The next morning, I jumped on a helicopter and was on my way north to Quang Tri. I landed, checked in, got issued combat gear, a rifle and a pistol, some new jungle boots and two days later, I was choppered out to "the bush."

I replaced a guy named Rolfing as the new S-2 scout for Delta Company, First Battalion, Third Marine Division. No more typewriters for me. I was with the grunts. I was good with that. Finally, I felt like a true Marine.

I walked point with three North Vietnamese scouts that were assigned to me. Lekien, Thom and

Tong. They'd been captured, rehabbed and sent back out to the field to assist with interrogation, detect ambushes and booby-traps and help guide us through the jungles.

I trusted them but not that much. They weren't working for America by choice. It hadn't been that long back, that they were trying to kill us.

I decided, from the get-go, that if I detected anything strange about their behavior, I'd kill them. When you're out there, scared, uptight and tense, survival consumes your brain. All you want is to get back home. You'll do whatever it takes to keep yourself alive.

Less than two months in-country, I took my first hit, May 5th, in the village of Dia Do. I bled a lot and thought I was gonna die. It wasn't that bad. I was medevaced out, got patched up and was back with the guys within a few days.

I'd written to my family and told them there was no reason for concern, that I was sitting behind a desk, "in the rear with the gear." I didn't want anybody to worry, especially Dad. He had just buried one of his sons. His heart was already broken enough.

I had no idea that whenever you get a Purple Heart that your family is informed. The same recruiter who signed me up, made a visit to Dad. My cover was blown. The recruiter made two more trips to tell Dad I'd been hit. Three "hearts" in less than nine months, and they sent me home.

About a year before Dad passed away, we were talking on the phone. I remember that we laughed a lot. Just before we hung up, he told me that he was proud of me and how worried for me he'd been, when I was in Vietnam.

I told him that he was the reason that I made it back, because I had been the best Marine that I could be. My father cried.

God, please bless all families with loved ones in the Armed Forces and pass on our respect and gratitude to those brave men and women, already up there with you, who gave their lives for our country.

And please tell all the Marines I said, "Happy Birthday."

And please, please continue to bless America.

TO ALL MY FELLOW VETERANS

There were over two-and-a-half million of us who showed up and kicked ass in Vietnam. Our homecoming wasn't pleasant. I got spit on and yelled at by a few guys. All of whom have my retaliation in the form of broken noses, loose teeth and permanent scars on their person. No way I was gonna take that after all I'd been through. I know that today should be one of pride and honor, and it is. But, I can't help it. It's also an angry day for me. God Bless all of those of you who have and are still fighting for our country's honor and sweet freedom...

        November 11, 2016 – Facebook

BELATED HAPPY BIRTHDAY TO THE MARINES AND HAPPY VETERAN'S DAY TO US ALL

When we stopped moving forward for the day, I'd walk back through the rice patties to join up with the rest of the troops and shoot the breeze, with the guys, over some dreadful C-rations and horrible military issued coffee.

I was an S-2 Scout and walked point for Delta Company, First Battalion, Third Marines, in Vietnam,

1968. I was in charge of three rehabilitated Viet Cong, who walked alongside me.

Thom, Tong and Lekian. All three had been high-ranking enemy soldiers. They'd come over to our side. They were razor-sharp in detecting enemy ambushes and booby traps. They assisted me with interrogations of villagers and captured Viet Cong or NVA. Good guys. Still, I only trusted them so far.

My fellow Marines and I had gone through some tough battles together. Including, making it through the Tet Offensive. We were brothers. We knew we could count on one another. All of us, proud members of the "Lean Green Fighting Machine." In as much as men can love one another, we did.

Most of us were nineteen or twenty years old. A bag of misfits, college dropouts and naïve kids. Almost all of us were drafted. Others, including myself, volunteered. Many of us had been "hit" once or twice. I remember thinking that it was gonna take a lot more than that to beat me. We all felt that way. We were young and proud Americans.

Usually, I was out in front of the rest of the battalion, by a couple hundred meters. Some Marine would run up to my position to let me know that we were stopping for the day.

As soon as I got back to the rest of the guys, on my way to a short briefing from Captain Fox, I'd hear the shout-outs. "Hey, Stamps, where we going tonight?"

I'd holler back, "We're on our way to the Sunset Strip, boys. See if we can't get next to some nasty girls at The Whiskey-A-Go-Go. It's gonna be a good night. I guarantee it!"

After we dug-in and cleared the perimeter, a bunch of us would get together and find a way to forget the horrors we had endured. We called ourselves The Dirty Dozen. Not terribly original, but that's roughly the number of us who hung out together.

There was Todd from Wisconsin. A short, red-haired guy. Glasses. Sun-burnt. Freckles all over. He flunked out of some Ivy League college, back East. They drafted him, shortly thereafter.

Pete, from Philly. His wife gave birth to his first child the second month he was "in country." A little girl. He tucked their picture, up front, under a black elastic band that ran around his helmet.

Mike, from Philadelphia. A blonde-haired, wanna-be surfer, with an attitude. The judge had told him, "It's jail or the service." He joined the Marines. He was quiet.

Zeke was from Wyoming. A real cowboy. Tall and skinny, with a gap between his two front teeth. He wrote to his fiancee every day. They were high school sweethearts. You couldn't get through a conversation with him without hearing all about her. He planned on marrying her, when he got back home.

There were several other guys in our group. A couple of them were from Texas. Two more from Alabama. A few others from all over.

Then, there was my best buddy, Paul. He, too, was from Philly. Short and stocky, with a Hollywood tan, a million-dollar smile, and a raspy voice. He walked with a slight limp. Paul was eight-or-nine years older than the rest of us. He had been in the Marine Corps for ten years and was on his second tour of Vietnam. He told me that as soon as he got back to the "world" he was getting out. In civilian life he had been a real-life pimp.

As many as twenty-five or thirty guys huddled up around us. Paul and I would stand up and start our show.

Paul would give me my lead, "Where are we Stamps?" I'd say, "We're standing in the middle of the bar at the Whiskey. There's a huge mirror above us. That way, we can see all the chicks in this place without having to turn around."

I'd continue, "Look in the mirror, Paul. We got it goin' on. Clean, man. My hair's long. Sideburns. Bell bottom jeans. I like my leather jacket, man. Red, with just a white, V-neck T-shirt underneath. You're lookin' good, Paul. Tanned. All dressed in black. Beatle boots. That gold chain around your neck's sparkling. That big gold watch. Your hair is just past your collar. You look clean as a dime, man."

Paul would look up, and into my imaginary mirror, and say, "Yeah man, we look good." Then me, "Hey, Paul. Look in the mirror. Check it out. Those girls are staring a hole through us. A whole table full!"

All the guys roared.

I continued, "Looks like they just came from the beach. That blonde, with more curves than the Ohio Turnpike, is smiling at you, Paul. This is gonna be a good night."

More approving cheers from our audience.

I'd say, "You take her, and I'll chat up the blonde, with the pony tail, next to her. I'd yell over the bar crowd, "Bartender, send over a round of drinks to those girls and tell them we'd like to get next to them, tonight."

Somebody would yell out, "What's the rest of the girls look like, Stamps?" I answered, "They're all good looking and horny for Marines. We're all getting lucky tonight, fellas!"

A big whoop from them. Fatigue and concern, set aside for the moment, to visualize my scenario and travel with me, back to the States. Loud cheers for "make believe." We all wanted to be home.

Sometimes, the show would go on for over an hour. That's the way it went on those hot and sweltering late afternoons over there. As the day drew to end, we'd dig in for the night and keep an eye on the horizon. We'd be lucky to get three hours of "shut-eye."

During a fire-fight, I was ten feet from Pete. I had to crawl on my belly from the horse shoe ambush we had walked into. I finally made it back behind a Vietnamese grave, where Pete was laying them out with his M60.

He looked at me, with that big toothy grin of his, and yelled out, "Where ya been, Stamps?" A minute later, they shot him right between the eyes.

Mike and Todd were fatally wounded by incoming mortar fire.

I watched Zeke stand straight up and just start walking toward incoming enemy fire. We were screaming at him, at the top of our lungs, to hit the ground. He just kept going. They blew him up. His fiancee had written him a "Dear John" letter. She had found another.

Shattered nerves and a broken heart was what really killed him.

All the rest of the guys in "The Dirty Dozen" died over there. I was the only one who made it. Or, so I thought. I had been told my buddy, Paul, had been killed too.

We lost track of one another. I got hit, and they choppered me out of the jungle. I never did catch back up with him.

Twenty-five years later, I found out Paul made it.

A friend of his family told me that Paul came home "all messed up." He just kind of wandered around the country, working odd jobs. He said that Paul had a drinking problem. The last he heard, Paul was living in upstate New York, working in the landscape business.

I looked around for him, for a while. I don't think he wants to be found. He probably doesn't want to talk about it. I understand. Me either.

Happy Veteran's Day. And, belated birthday wishes to my fellow Marines. Gentlemen and ladies, celebrate the freedom you've protected. Thank God that you're alive . . .

DUFFY

(This Memorial Day, we honor our fellow Americans who willingly and courageously mounted up and deployed to far away lands and gave their lives for our continued freedom. Before you pop one open or flip a burger...before your backyard festivities begin...put your hand over your heart, bow your head and give thanks to Heaven for our courageous, fallen service men and women...God's favorite angels.)

When you get hit, two things happen. You hear the crack and feel the thud. In my case, shrapnel, white-hot and razor-sharp. At first, it just stings. Then a fire, from within, ignites. It's hard not to scream. It just keeps burning.

All five senses go on high-end alert. Even with all your combat training and the brainwashing they preach to you about how Marines should conduct themselves under enemy fire, you're still scared to death.

The impact of the projectile is deafening. Your body goes into shock immediately following the hit. Then, the penetration into your skin. Once you've come to the realization that you've been wounded, you start looking for the blood. Try to patch it up. Stop the bleeding. Seeing a part of your body ripped open can be nauseating. But, you have to see where it went in, in order to wrap the hit properly.

Then, "fight to live" kicks in.

You don't have much time to fool around with your wound. There's still a "fire fight" going on. They're trying to get to you. To kill you. If you're able, you honker down and pick them off, as they run toward you. I hate saying so, but there's a kind of rush you feel, when you shoot and see him go down.

I've actually screamed out loud, a jubilant "Yeah, Baby," as I've watched the guy die, just out in front of me. I've asked God, a million times, to please forgive me for having had those feelings. I'm holding onto the hope that the Almighty, somehow, will give me a pass. I was taught that God is very forgiving. I truly hope so. Otherwise, I doubt I'll see you on the other side.

After you've gotten back into a prone position and begin firing back, you can't help it, tears start rolling down. Unstoppable.

They're not the kind you have when your feelings get hurt. They're more like tears Satan might cry. A mixture of fear, anger and an uncontrollable despise for another human being. You grit your teeth and through the blur of the tears, you give it all you've got to make them suffer and die.

Not the way I was brought up. There went my Christianity.

After awhile, you can actually taste the metal in your body. The smell of your own skin burning. If you don't watch it, the magnitude and weight of it all can get the better of you. Never panic. Push yourself to go on the offensive. Again, numero uno is to survive. Stay alive and go home.

I had thought that I was up in the front by myself. I was an S2 Scout. I walked point. When the stuff hit the fan, I was usually stuck in the crossfire. I'd hit the ground and belly-crawl back to my guys. This day, all of us were pretty much pinned down. There was nowhere to go. I found cover behind a Vietnamese grave.

The Vietnamese farmers bury their kin out in the rice patties. The more important the person was, the higher they built a knoll above the grave. I don't eat white rice.

All of a sudden, to my right, there's Duffy. He had made his way to the front line because he wanted to "take the fight to them." He had that reputation. I'd seen him around and had said hello. That was about it. Out of the blue and over the noise and chaos, he yelled to me, "Don't worry about nothin'. We got God on our side." Then a big grin.

We were no more than 10 feet apart.

He was a lanky-built, country-raised, Baptist boy out of Tuscaloosa, Ala., with a few more months left on his second tour. Like me, he wore a fu manchu moustache. He had crooked teeth and glaring eyes. He had been "in country" long enough, that he had gone native.

Duffy got hit first. Then me. He took it in the leg. Me, my back and foot.

I crawled over to help him tie a makeshift tourniquet around his thigh. He wasn't bleeding that much. I had just gotten through telling him that his wound didn't look that bad, and then I got hit. I couldn't believe it.

After the smoke cleared, Duffy gave me a quick glance and started firing back. I took off my boot and wrapped my foot with my sock. Duffy was shooting and hollering at them and screaming like a mad man.

Crazy as it sounds, watching him get after them like that, cracked me up. He was full-blown. Here we were, wounded and in pain. Bullets whizzing. Grenades. And, of all things, I couldn't stop laughing. Duffy started laughing, too. Then, we relocked-and-loaded and lit it up!

It's an understatement to say that you really get to know a guy in combat situations. Things happen so fast that one has only his instinct on which to rely. A man's pride and what courage he has shows up. The fear goes away. You get it in your mind that you're going to fight till the end. You just kinda throw it all to the wind.

Duffy was a walking contradiction. He carried a little black Bible in his backpack, could quote the Scriptures, and believed that God had wanted him to join the Marines and volunteer for Vietnam. He told me his mama had received the same message from the Lord. Duffy felt that he was on a mission for God. Yet, he was one sadistic son-of-a-gun. Somewhere between crazy and out of his mind.

We became friends.

Duffy and I were medivaced out on the same chopper back to Dong Ha. But, he went one way and me the other. He didn't come back out to the field. Nobody seemed to know what happened to him.

A few months later, my unit was choppered up to Cambodia, just over the border, to meet up with another group of Marines and help protect an artillery battery. Nixon was denying our troops were there. We made camp and dug in on a cleared-out knoll parallel to the big guns.

A Marine helicopter, attempting to deliver food, water, ammo and medical supplies to us, was shot out of the sky and tumbled, head-over-tea-kettle, down the side of the mountain and into the valley below.

It would take them three long days to make a successful drop.

In the meantime, they rationed out the water. It tasted like what you get out of a garden hose on a hot summer day. Add the malaria pills, and it tastes like you're drinking swimming pool water.

When you haven't eaten for three days, even C-rations sound good.

You can't call C-rations real food, per say. Vacuum sealed stuff, in drab green, tin cans left over from World War ll. Beans with frankfurter chunks in tomato sauce, beef in spiced sauce, beef slices with potatoes and gravy, and the worst of the bunch, ham and lima beans. We called it ham and mother#*#*#. It's awful stuff. Just a little better than prison meals.

I remember thinking that if those starving kids in Africa, that my grandmother used to tell me about, when I didn't want to eat something on my plate, were offered a big helping of C-rations, they would have said, "no thanks."

I could have sold a hamburger over there for a hundred bucks!

Came the next morning of our arrival, and we were hot, tired, thirsty and hungry. Being up on that knoll gave us no shade. I was told to clean my rifle and get ready to go on patrol that night. I'm pulling gauze through the barrel and up walks Duffy. And, his big grin. We huddled up and talked the day away.

Duffy's plan for when he returned to "the world" was a simple one. Get a part-time job outside of the base they next sent him to. Serve out the year he would have left in the Corps. Go back home and put a down payment on a dairy farm.

He was convinced that being a dairy farmer was what God wanted him to do. So was his mother. She was going to move out of Duffy's older sister's home and come live with him. He had great love for his mother. She lived by the Bible. Duffy doubted his mom would ever marry again.

Furthermore, he had a theory that having cows around would keep him calm. Such was the case when his father had abruptly left and never came back. It was just him and his mom. He told me that milking their cows had relaxed him.

Day 2 of nothing to eat. I had a plan. Get permission from Captain Fox for me to go outside the perimeter and shoot a rock ape. They're about four feet tall and kinda look like miniature gorillas. More tan in color. They were running all over the place.

I had found an old piece of tin. Just perfect for grilled "T-Bone Monkey." Duffy agreed to chop it up and cook it. We both reckoned that rock ape probably tasted like chicken. I remember Duffy saying, in his nasal-twanged Alabama drawl, "It kain't taste no worse than squirrel."

I shot a good-sized ape within minutes.

After the fire got going, the monkey pieces started cooking. The smell ran across the top of the hill. In fact, it smelled like chicken ... kinda. Duffy was flipping the meat and whistling. We were on to something. Not long from now, he and I and some of our chosen few were gonna be chowing down on some monkey meat, that was, hopefully, going to taste like chicken.

A crowd gathered. Duffy cut off a piece and stuck it in his mouth. While he was chewing it, he smiled and said, "Not bad." Hallelujah! Jubilantly, I yelled out, "Let the feast begin!"

I took a bite and swallowed it. It tasted as though the monkey was still alive. It was like ingesting stench. The glob hit my stomach and was on its way back up. The same for the chosen few. We all engaged in synchronized, projectile erping. In between their internal eruptions, the guys were cursing me. It went on for a while.

Duffy never got sick. And, from time to time, he went back over to the tin and nibbled. Iron guts, those Southern Baptists.

The next day, just before dusk, they made the supplies drop. We were starving. Even ham and lima beans sounded good. For the rest of the time I was in Vietnam, they didn't let me forget about the monkey meal. Duffy was rotated back to the states a little before me. We lost touch. I called every Duffy in

Tuscaloosa, years ago. It was difficult, in that I never knew his first name. No telling where he ended up.

Knowing Duffy, he got that farm and some cows. He's probably buried his mom by now. I don't know why, but I get the feeling that he's by himself.

Sitting on his front porch and watching people go by. They may look over at him and see an aging man. He may have put on a few pounds. There's probably nothing about him that shows signs of the pure warrior he was known to be. Unless you get up close. Close enough to see that glare in his eyes.

Hey, Duffy. If you're out there, I hope you've been having a good life. If you ever get to feeling a little down, or if the demons show up, don't worry about nothin'. We got God on our side...

REMEMBERING ALL OUR HEROES THIS MEMORIAL DAY

I've only written a few stories about my tour in Vietnam. It goes without saying, that it wasn't a fun time in my life. When I signed up with the Marines, I had full intentions of going over there and kicking their butts all the way back up to Hanoi. I was actually looking forward to it. I know that sounds crazy, and it was. What did I know? I was eighteen.

My MOS, (military occupational specialty) was Intelligence. I've never figured that one out. I barely made it out of high school. Little did I know what lay ahead for me. Some of it's been good, some of it, not so much. I'd say it's been close to 50-50.

The good has been really good. An exciting forty years in the entertainment business. All the monetary trappings. Meeting and working with a bunch of famous people. More than I ever imagined, when I lay on my back on green grass Tennessee hilltops, daydreaming the afternoons away. Everything was ahead of me. All was well for this country boy.

I'm, now, of the age that a lot of my life is in the rearview mirror. Memories of decades that have passed through time, with me at the wheel. Rather than daydreaming, I now remember.

I've definitely taken some wrong turns. Many of them uphill and bumpy. I've had my share of dead ends. A few times, I took off heading for what I thought was going to be a fabulous journey, only to find myself back at where I began.

I've had good fortune on many fronts. I have a son. Twenty-three years ago, I bumped into my wife, Jana. Somehow, she saw through my veneer and decided to love me, warts and all. I met her at an emotionally crippling time in my life. There's not enough space on this page to explain it all. Jana saved me from myself.

Funny thing about showbiz. They don't care about your bad habits or your soul. Just bring home the bacon, get handsomely rewarded and carry on. The system worked perfectly for me. I'd already done it that way before.

When I got back from Nam, there were no ticker tape welcome home parades. Nobody gave a good damn about where you'd been or what you'd been through. Booze and drugs were my "go to." I learned to suck it up and carry on. To keep it to myself in a pent-up-ready-to-explode container, that I tucked deep down inside.

Consequently, there were several guys, thinking they were cute, who found themselves picking up their teeth from the floor. I'm not proud of any of that. It was a full-time job for me to stay in control of myself. Sometimes, it still is. PTSD is no joke.

After boot camp, 2nd ITR, and Guerilla Warfare School, my first military assignment was to the Fifth Engineers Battalion, at the far most western tip of Camp Pendleton, California. Camp Telega. Half the guys there were coming back from Vietnam and awaiting their Honorable Discharge papers. Most of the rest of us were waiting to go.

It was great suffering for a guy like me, being stuck behind a typewriter, pecking out Secret Clearances for "lifers." Men who stay in the service for twenty years or more. Here I am, the guy who wanted to go to Vietnam, doing secretary work. No man, worth his salt, wants to sit "in the rear with the gear." For a Marine, it's kinda like sitting on the bench at the World Series.

At Camp Telega, there were five of us in the Intelligence Department. Lt. Johnson, my commanding officer, who was awaiting his overseas orders. Two Staff Sergeants. One of them had done a tour in Nam and came back crazy. The other one, Staff Sergeant Brown, was a "lifer" and gave me a hard time. He didn't look like a Marine. More like Barney Fife on the TV show, "Mayberry RFD." I doubt he weighed 110 soaking wet.

Then, there was Sergeant Marshall, who'd been in the Corps for ten or so years and wanted nothing to do with Vietnam. He told me that he intended to do everything he could to skip the war. He used to say, "Stamps, I don't want to be a dead hero. I have my family to think about." I understood.

A gold framed picture of his high school, sweetheart wife and their two young blonde haired boys sat on his desk, next to a plaque with little Marine Corps and American flags stuck in it and his engraved name on the front.

More than a few times, Sergeant Marshall came to my rescue from Staff Sergeant Brown's disapproval of my job performance. I didn't type worth a flip. I couldn't get through three lines without making a mistake. I went through enough whiteout to paint a barn. Administrative matters were not my calling. To this day, I type with just two fingers.

Between Staff Sergeant Brown always on me and my pride, I was at wits' end. I kept volunteering for Vietnam every chance I got. Almost a year went by. Nothing. I found out that I'd been passed over twice, because the Base Commanding Officer, Major Hines, didn't want to lose me as his handball partner. I told him how much I wanted to go. That I just couldn't bear to sit out the war.

Within a few weeks, I was on my way to Staging, preparing to go to Vietnam. I was raring to go. Sadly, out of the blue, my 16 year old brother, Ricky, fell off a cliff and died. The Red Cross people sent me home to be with my family.

Three weeks, from the day we buried my favorite brother, I was in Vietnam. At night, in a foxhole, out in the jungle, thousands of miles away from home, it caught up with me. I gave it all I had to hide my tears from the guys. I found a way to use my extreme sorrow as a weapon. I became a viscous person. I did things, over there, that I'll never tell.

About six months in-country, a double dose of malaria and two Purple Hearts later, I was back walking point, when we took enemy fire. We had unknowingly walked into a horseshoe ambush. They have three sides of you surrounded. When a good many Marines are within the "U", they open fire.

Crossfire is a whole other kind of combat. I've seen young men's bodies severed in two from bullets simultaneously coming at us from every direction. More than one war historian has said that Vietnam is, by far, the goriest war of them all. Any guy who was there will concur. Human beings aren't meant to see so much devastation. So much death. It stays with you.

As always, I hit the ground and began my crawl out. You keep your head as close to the ground as you can. However, my peripheral vision enabled me to guide my crawl out by marking my distance from a tree line or something else, like a ditch. You just keep on crawling. Sometimes, crawling over a dead Marine. One of my brothers.

After most of the day and into the night, we killed as many North Vietnamese as we could. They finally retreated. Just after dawn, we began to bag up the mortally wounded and prepare LZs, landing zones, for the choppers. Throughout the day, they kept landing, picking up the dead and wounded and leaving. We had suffered great losses.

I was having a cigarette with a few Marines, waiting to load up more body bags into choppers, when I heard someone behind me, zipping up a body bag, say, "They got Sergeant Marshall." I got a pain in my gut. I walked over there and unzipped the bag a little. It was him. My friend. I had no idea that he was in-country. I lost it. All I could think of was that picture, on his desk, of his wife and two little boys.

One of the guys said that Sergeant Marshall was attempting to carry a Marine out of the line of fire, when he took a bullet to the heart. He said that Sergeant Marshall was known for his cool demeanor during fire fights. He died a hero.

So, this Memorial Day I'll be thinking of Sergeant Marshall and all the other brave men who went to war and gave their lives for our country. Whether or not you agree with the Vietnam War, there's no denying the courage of 58,220 dead American heroes, including Sergeant Marshall. God bless their souls.

Say a prayer for our American warriors out there somewhere in harm's way and remember, there's more to Memorial Day than stuff on sale.

ENDURING THOUGHTS AT 3 AM

I sure wish I could figure out what to do with all this junk in my head. It's come back. It never really went away.

I just crowded my life up with project after project. Set goals and made plans to do things. It was just enough to keep the bad stuff down in a hole in my mind. I'm getting older and doing less. It's becoming harder to keep it away. I'm sure there must be a trick to get rid of, at least, some of the visuals.

They told us it was mosquito repellent. They used to drop it right on top of us sometimes. I don't remember what we called it in Nam, but it wasn't Agent Orange. I've read about its symptoms and characteristics. I have them all.

It's a weird thing, getting shot at. It's something else to get hit. First, it's just a big crack and a thud. Then, it's like somebody set a fire inside you. You can't put it out. You can be the baddest Marine in the land, but you can't stop the scream. Then, you realize you're alive. Then, you start looking for the wound. For me, it was my feet, back, butt, head, arm and knee.

I'm all healed up now, physically. But, I can look at the scars and remember what it looked like when it happened. It can still make me dizzy.

For years after I came home, little pieces of shrapnel came out of my back and butt. Hurt like Hell.

Malaria is something else. Spiking temperatures and then down to under 97 degrees. You hallucinate. When the nurses were cooling me down, by dumping ice on my naked body and running fans on me, I saw a waterfall falling from my brain to my feet.

I caught malaria twice. I had two relapses in my 20s.

For decades, I've worked hard. I've achieved some degree of success. I've made a lot of friends over the years. I don't know where most of them went. Never tried to keep up. I was too busy being by myself.

Don't know where a lot of my money went, either. Booze and drugs have been close associates of mine for decades. Sometimes, they were my best friends. They seemed to understand what I was going through. I stopped all that awhile back. Sometimes I miss them, but I know that I can't afford to allow them to come back around.

We did have a helluva time together. So people have told me. A Hollywood Bad Boy, they used to call me. At the time, I kinda liked the title. Jail is a horrible and humbling place to end up after a night out on the town.

Confinement drives me out of my mind. It doesn't pay to get into fights with inmates. They make you stay longer.

I never had a death wish, but you wouldn't know it by the way I drove my cars. Who totals four sports cars and walks away unscathed?

I recently let God come into my life. I saw Him grimace when he opened me up. There was a mess of sin in there. When I was younger, I figured he didn't want much to do with me. I didn't blame him.

I don't hunt. I know many guys who do. To me, it's like ambushing an innocent one of God's creations. Have you ever looked closely at a bird's feathers? When I was a child, I was told that God personally sat down and hand-painted them, himself. Just can't imagine he took all that time on them to be shot for sport.

After you've shot and killed other men, hunting is not something you care anything about. It's hard to believe that we used to keep score over there.

I hate loud noises, including loud people. I've been feeling that there's something wrong with me for a long time. I assume it's to do with my childhood, and Vietnam.

Like I said, God just got here. We've had some talks. Between Him and Jana, I'm thinking everything's gonna work out alright.

I hope they find a cure for war someday. It puts a real dent in your life.

By the way, I don't feel sorry for myself. It could be a lot worse. I have a childhood friend from Cleveland who suffers daily from his memories of Vietnam.

I'm hoping all this suffering has not gone unnoticed by The Almighty.

Please God, bless us all.

CHAPTER II

BILL'S LAST STORIES . . . AND PERSONAL COMMENTARY

This second chapter is comprised of some of the last stories Bill wrote. Some just prior to us leaving for a 6-month stint to California. The rest of them when we returned to Tennessee, September 2020.

On our long journey back from California, when we thought we might perish from the intense heat of the Texas desert as our air conditioning stopped working, I told Bill I would kiss the ground when we crossed the border-line into Tennessee. I missed doing so that day, but once we got back to Cleveland, I got down on my knees and kissed the green grass and soil and thanked the Almighty for bringing us back home.

The trip was excruciating. We saw the walking dead in Phoenix. Those poor souls who looked like they had just crossed the border. Men and women wandering the streets, in what looked like a state of shock and trauma, rummaging through the trash.

Then, there was that huge pig in a cage in the back of a trailer. A young woman doing her best to douse him in water. The conditions were atrocious. She looked like she was on her last legs too. There's no doubt that animal was suffering even though she was giving it all she had. There was nothing I could do but bear witness to the sadness and that gut-punch feeling of desolation in your soul. Not to mention the many stories of either desperate or inhumane people who choose to put their pets in the back of the truck only to find them dead on arrival from heat and suffocation. By the thousands every year.

When we decided to go out to California, we had just lost our last pet, Scout. Heartbroken is not even remotely close to the loss we felt. Scout meant so much to us. He was my little helper. He kept Bill going. He represented a pillar in our life. I would pray for Scout to live as long as Bill.

Bill was run down. So was I. We both needed a break. He'd been writing a new story every week for the better part of 5 years, with no pay. He felt like he had nothing left to write. Had given it all he had.

Few would ever venture down this road. Every story Bill wrote took a piece of him, often ripping his soul to shreds with memories he tried to bury a long time ago. He did this over 150 times.

Bill was blessed with his phenomenal mind. A unique, God-given ability to write as though he were talking to you. He would enter a form of trance and fend off the demons of his mind to access the soul's memory. His uncanny ability to remember dialogue and episodes in his life is as close to brilliant as I have ever witnessed.

I am the only one in the unique position to know all that Bill endured to bring life to his stories. To entertain his readers. He chose mainly to write about the good stuff.

Except these. There's no sugar-coating Vietnam.

IN MEMORY OF BILL STAMPS

By William Wright

When I first met Bill Stamps at a radio station there was an inexplicable ease about the way he looked at me, spoke to me, behaved around me and I quickly realized that this was a man after my own heart. Bill was as unpretentious a person as I had met. He was always a gentleman, tactful yet outspoken. I was interviewing him for a personality profile in the Cleveland Daily Banner, but I had no idea who he was, the experiences had, the places he'd been, the celebrities he'd met, the wars he fought or the past that made him one of the most interesting human beings anyone could ever meet. Suffice to say, Bill was an open book. He shared his truth — the good, the bad and the ugly — and he did so admiringly. You couldn't help but love the guy for his candor and courage to tell it like it is.

Over the years we spoke more over the phone than in person, and I always appreciated our conversations that touched on race, because I felt Bill's background helped him understand what was difficult to put into words unless you lived it. Bill understood people. He understood social injustice, inequality and he expressed his hatred of it. This was between me and him, mind you. We were revealing who we truly were and what we truly thought because that had become the level of our friendship. I was comfortable listening to him, his experiences and personal views and we bonded the only way soul brothers could bond. We talked about everything. As a writer and communicator, he had the most wonderful words! He was eloquent even when describing himself being inebriated or incarcerated earlier in life.

Yet, it was his admiration for his adoring wife, Jana, that I felt defined the man I had come to know as Bill Stamps. His honesty about the woman behind the man — the lady who loved him back to life, helped him heal and hope again — Jana was his life and one true love. He praised her in her presence and behind her back. To me, this spoke volumes about a man who finally understood what life was all about — to love and be loved in return. Bill had come full circle and embraced the simple pleasures of a life filled with love. I knew he had regrets. Like all of us, he did too. I believe he made peace with them the best that he could. Now that he is gone I will miss not having spent more time in his company.

For me, I will find much of Bill in the soul music he loved. The music he played on his morning radio program was the absolute best! It told me so much about the man before I ever met him! Bill was full of soul. He was white chocolate, a brother from another mother and a brother like no other. The fact that he had been a scout while serving in combat in the Marine Corps in Vietnam, watching many friends die in battle, seeing others neglected and abused upon their return, and living with those haunting memories of war, make Bill's compassion and composure all the more remarkable. He was someone you could talk to because you knew he'd understand. He'd listen and he wouldn't judge. That was my experience with Bill Stamps. He was cool. He was loved... and he will be missed.

IN RECOGNITION OF MY BEST FRIEND

I hope you won't mind me breaking from my format so that I can tell you about my love for our dog, Scout. He's on his last legs.

Just over fourteen years ago, my wife, Jana, and I took delivery of two Australian Shepherd puppies. Blue Merles. We picked them from a championship breeder out of Orange County, California. Two boys.

Cowboy and Scout. They were born on the same day, they just came out different.

Scout was the runt of the litter. For most of his life, he's been a sport model. He actually has a sense of humor. He has one brown eye and the other eye is half-blue and half-brown. Every time I look over his way, he's staring at me with his little happy eyes.

Scout's pleased to meet anyone. He greets all people, men and women, the same way. The old nose in the crotch salutation.

Wait, there's more. When he's through with his frontal assault, he heads for the backsides of these poor people and does some more investigatory sniffing. It's hard to pull him away. Of course, the people always say not to worry about it. They say, "Don't worry about it. He's fine."

But, both of us know, not really. The longer Scout does that, the more difficult it is to carry on a conversation with the victim. I usually try to cut the conversation short and hope that I can get down the road before they notice the wet smudges. It's embarrassing. But, in a little bitty way, it's embarrassingly funny.

Cowboy was a big boy. A head taller than Scout. He looked like a movie star. He was big and muscular and extremely loyal. Especially to Jana. When he was full-speed running, he looked like a lion running down his prey. His "see deep into your soul" big eyes were white blue. Wolf eyes. Cowboy was a lover.

A year later, we got one more pup from the same breeder. Same mom, different sire. He was a thinner version of Cowboy and kinda picky as to whom he let get close to him. We named him Chief. He couldn't get enough love. He'd jump up on the couch and lay right up next to me. If I dared stop rubbing his back, he'd stick his nose under my elbow and nudge it over and over, until I pet him some more.

At night, all three of the boys slept around our bed. Cowboy on Jana's side, Chief at the foot of the bed and Scout on my side. To this day, Scout still sleeps right next to me on his special rug.

Once-in-a-while, I wake up and check to make sure he's still breathing. He's a pretty sound sleeper. Just to make sure he's ok, I'll give him a little shake. He looks at me funny. Poor Scout could probably get more sleep in a hospital.

I know that any of you who have or have had a dog know just how much you end up loving them. When they go, it's like losing a close member of the family. I'm not sure why God doesn't let them live longer. One day, they're just fine, and the next day, they can't get up. It's heart breaking.

We lost Chief a little over three years ago. He was 10 and still acting like a puppy. His passing caught us completely off guard. Chief was fast as lightning and could jump high into the back of our Range Rover. He had that twisted-stomach thing. It was terribly sad. We were back to the original two. Cowboy and Scout.

Early one morning, a little over a year ago, Cowboy couldn't move. He tried. He lay there and just looked at me with those big, beautiful, blue eyes. I didn't realize at the time, it was his goodbye look. We rushed him to the vet. It was too late. Cancer. Within an hour, Cowboy was gone. Jana and I were devastated.

Scout is the last one standing. For at least a week, he was looking through the house and out in the yard for Cowboy. They hadn't missed a day, since birth, being together. It was desperately sad to see Scout trying to find his brother. The loss of love is so very painful.

Jana, the strongest of the two of us, got over it sooner than I. It's probably the Swiss in her. I was the one sitting up late and blubbering. I can deal with the sometime harshness of reality on almost any front. Not so well, when it comes to the heart. Plus, I was feeling deep empathy for Jana. She so loved Cowboy. They had a special bond.

A few months ago, Scout had two seizures within twenty minutes of each other. Each of them lasted a minute or so. I've never witnessed a dog having a seizure. Scared me to death. Word to the wise, give them ice cubes. When they come out of it, they need to cool down as quickly as possible.

He lost all of his hearing and some of his vision. He has a hard time getting up and has a lump or two on his body. He moves a lot slower these days. He kinda reminds me of me. He doesn't appear to be in pain. So, we're going to let him live out the rest of his remaining life with no operations.

Since his two brothers crossed the bridge, Scout receives all the attention. Some of the house rules have been relaxed. Used to be, the pups weren't allowed in the kitchen. All three of them would lie right at the doorway and watch Jana cook. That rule has flown out the window.

These days, Scout couldn't be any more under Jana's feet. He considers himself to be in a kitchen supervisorial position. We don't care anymore. Scout has the run of the house and us wrapped around his little paw.

Scout and I are night owls. Plus, he knows that he can count on me for a midnight snack or two. He lives to eat. Some canine dietary purists may get after me, but Scout's already made it to old. I'm pretty sure if he could talk, he'd say, "Dad, don't give this balanced diet thing a second thought. Why don't we tippy-toe into the kitchen and heat up those enchiladas Mom put in the refrigerator? We'll split 'em."

As much as I love Scout and him me, I'm almost certain that if I was hanging from a cliff and needed him to bring me a rope, and there was a hamburger close by, I'd be a goner. He can't help himself when it comes to hamburgers. He's partial to Logans.

We changed Scout's diet. Now, he eats like dogs that were owned by farming families, back in the day. Leftovers. Jana separates the foods that aren't good for him. So now, our little boy chows down on vegetables, eggs, beef stew, steak bones and left over grits. He can't get enough. At least, he'll leave this world happy.

My childhood dog, Prince, lived to be almost 16. Scout reminds me of him. Every morning, Prince was fed a can of Kennel Ration. Besides that, he climbed up in my lap and helped me with my morning cereal, lunch-time sandwiches and whatever was for supper. We both ate out of the same bowl or plate.

Sharing, with those I love, has always come naturally to me.

Scout turned 14 this past April. I know his time is limited. I don't know how I'm going to be able to take his departure. It's gonna kill me. He has my heart. He's special to me. He started showing me extra love at a very low point in my life. I love Scout more than a lot of people I know. Maybe, even most.

Chief and Cowboy have been added to my list of loved ones, no longer with us, that I think about every day and include in my nightly prayers. Happy thoughts and memories can turn to sad, if I don't watch it. I'm not sure when I started getting so sappy. They say as you get older, you get more sentimental. That's probably it. In dog years, I'm 490.

Our pets deserve to be treated with love and respect. They live to make you happy and receive your praise. When you think about it, that's very powerful. Never take them for granted. They won't be around forever.

It seems like it wasn't that long ago that my grandmother, Miz Lena, told me, "Honey Baby, life don't stop and wait fer yuh." Grand Mom, you were so right. Please God, let our little Scout live a few more years. I'll gladly give up a few of mine, and we'll call it even.

DEAR GOD,

THANK YOU FOR CREATING WATER

I can't help what pops into my brain. If you took a peek in there, I'm pretty sure, at the very least, you'd say, "Oh my Lord!" Sometimes, I feel like my mind needs to be drained. I'd rather run a quart low than overflow.

I have an exercise that helps keep me stable. It's a mental workout. Any time I have a less-than-pleasant thought or one of those bad, bad memories, I look around for beauty and concentrate on it. It's like pumping fresh air into a room filled with smoke.

I've never taken Mother Nature's ambience for granted. I thank my lucky stars that I spent the first thirteen years of my complex life in the South, and at least half of those years growing up out in the country, in the '50s, when things and people and the universe were at peace.

It's not as if everything was perfect, back then. But as a child, it seemed pretty perfect to me. The best part of being a kid is that you don't give a flip what's going on in the rest of the world. You have your very own agenda.

Every day is a brand, spanking, new one, custom made for kids. It felt as though the waking morning lay in wait for me, right outside my front door. A bowl of Cheerios, my five-minutes-or-less "commode duty", and I was gone. My dog, Prince, and I ran with the rising sun in pursuit of adventure and, ultimately, a full day's worth of happiness.

All colors on God's pallet are mixed with water.

In the country, all around you are colors. More colors than you can shake a stick at. God took his time when he painted Tennessee. It's some of his best work. Like all the different hues of green that he used to color our world.

Nothing's more beautiful than the first buds of green leaves on soggy trees after the coldness moves out and makes way for early Spring's brighter days. Fresh-cut pastures and gardens of new-birth vegetables add to the mix.

Flowers of all colors and fragrances are right in front of us. I grew up around roses and iris flowers. If I concentrate, I can smell my grandmother's pink, yellow and red blooming rose garden teaming with soft honeysuckle and permeating through musky Summer nights. More fresh air for my very smoky mind.

For years, before moving back to Tennessee, I lived by the ocean, in Southern California. It's magical from sunup to sunset.

I miss the morning sounds of the beach. When those waves begin to come in, in melodic sets of four, there's no doubt in my mind that the Almighty's running the show.

We can't live without water.

It's a downright shame, what they're doing to our oceans and streams. They waved off preservation in favor of profit and went to plastic. Now, all these years later, there are islands of plastic, the size of a city, floating around out there in our oceans.

It must make God sad enough to cry, seeing his vision and creativity being destroyed by mankind. Those corporate "muckity-mucks" will have to answer up to Him for daring to dismantle and ruin what was perfect.

When they first started selling plastic bottles of water, I thought that was the silliest thing I'd ever heard. Who, in their right mind, was gonna pay for free water and then drink it out of plastic containers? Certainly, not us Southerners.

Of course, many years back, I was positive that when Coca Cola converted from glass bottles to cans, that it wasn't gonna fly. I was wrong.

When I was a little "whipper-snapper" I could just run in, stick my head under the kitchen faucet and the water was pure. In the winter, it came out the faucet cold as ice.

Or, you could open up the fridge. Most everyone had a glass pitcher of cold water, that came from the faucet, sitting in there next to the milk. I remember my grandmother, Miz Lena, setting out glasses of ice-water with our meals.

They started adding chemicals to it and the water began to taste like a swimming pool. Not too long later, they started selling water to us. Not just one brand, but several. I always thought water was water. I guess I was wrong.

The best tasting water I've ever had came from a spring on Mr. Mullin's farm, in the little country town, in which I lived, over in Middle Tennessee.

The water babbled right out of the earth and flowed into a nature-built basin, then emptied into a creek that ran all the way back into town. No matter the seasonal temperature, that spring water was always cold.

Three or four times a day, one of the many Mullin kids would step out the back kitchen door with a big, two-gallon oak bucket, walk back to the spring and fill it to the brim. With both hands on the handle, they stiff-leg-walked and sloshed the bucket of water back to the house.

All you country boys and girls know that a bucket of water is plenty heavy. Little country kids, sent to fetch water, got strong at an early age.

As a matter of fact, you didn't want to get into it with a Mullin's gal. They all had muscles. The fourth-grader, Betty, especially. I was a grade behind her. It was apparent that she was kinda sweet on me.

She was always chasing me, trying to kiss me. I was faster. Still, she got me once in a while. After a few kisses from her, I started feeling a special tingle in my belly.

I must admit, as the day went on, I'd slow down and let her catch me. She always caught me the same way. She tackled me like a linebacker. There was no prim and proper with Betty. Still, she was a pretty good kisser.

When the cold months came, spots along the creek froze over. The Mullin's spring slowed to a trickle. Ice cycles hung from the limbs of the birch trees rooted above the spring and less than a stone's throw from the creek. Those were the best ice cycles I ever bit into. We called them, God's popsicles.

Out in the country, there's a code, an unwritten law, when it comes to water. Drink it, use it, but don't waste it.

I think country folks have a better appreciation for water than do city slickers. Maybe, if those urbanites had had to fetch a bucket or two, they'd think twice about emptying out a perfectly good glass of water. If I have a little left over, I look for a plant to pour it in.

Aside from farmers, all combat veterans appreciate water. Ask any guy who's been pinned down for hours, with the sweltering sun right over the top of them, how much a precious swig of water is appreciated.

I hate to admit it, but one of my valor ribbons the Marine Corps awarded me, wasn't about heroism. It was about water.

We fought all day and were honkered down behind some Vietnamese graves, awaiting artillery back up. Snipers were in the trees, waiting for us to raise our heads. It was hot. So hot, that your sweat dried up as soon as it came out.

Generally, most of us carried as many canteens of water, on our cartridge belts, that we could. Water is fuel for warriors. Even if you have self-discipline and ration yourself, that water goes fast.

I looked out in front of me and saw a dead Marine, lying on his belly, no more than thirty yards away. I could see that he had several canteens on his belt. We were completely out. Over there, staying hydrated is super important. If you're not careful, that sun can suck the life out of you.

I decided that I'd go get that water. I took off my helmet, backpack and flack jacket, said a prayer, got down into my running stance and took off. It's hard to run in jungle boots but when they're shooting at you, you'd be surprised how fast you can get to the thirty-yard line.

I got there and reached down to unbuckle his cartridge belt and heard, "Oh, thank God." The Marine was alive. He'd been lying perfectly still so the snipers wouldn't shoot him, again. He'd taken one in his back.

They were firing all around me. Without hesitation, and with some kind of strength that God must have given me for that very moment, I clean-jerked him up on my shoulders and ran back to the grave. No doubt in my mind, God covered me.

Jesus' birthday is less than three weeks away. If you want to give him a present that's sure to please him, in your next prayer, make a vow to protect his father's greatest creation. Water.

A WHOLE NEW DECADE TO GET IT RIGHT

My grandmother, Miz Lena, used to tell me, "If you don't like who yuh are, yore liable to die unhappy and early."

This time of the year, I do some internal soul searching. I ask myself pretty much the same questions every year. Am I where I want to be? Am I happy? Am I contributing? I make a vow to not make the same mistakes again, and I try to forgive those who have done me wrong.

Now's the time to begin to discard the "uglies" and clear the clogs. Sorta like that Drano TV commercial. Remember the one that shows a plugged up clear pipe that eventually unclogs and fresh water flushes through it? Like that.

Just as there are two sides to every story, I believe that we all have more than one person inside. It's not a hard one to figure out. We're never the same way all the time.

Sometimes, we're happy, sometimes sad. Some days anxious, other times patient. My favorite me is calm and collected. The goal is to stay that way. In this world, at this particular time, it's tough to do.

Having been in the entertainment business for close to forty years, I learned to never let them see me sweat, even if my insides were burning.

I don't know why, but there's a certain kind of person that sees you struggling and waits for first signs of weakness, then pounces. I don't care for these types of people. To my way of thinking, they're cowards. Cowards have no heart or conscience.

Most cowards are bullies. Used to be, not that long ago, I took a certain pleasure in smacking bullies around on behalf of their victims.

I've always felt that it's important for bullies to taste the same pain (and then some) that they've inflicted on the weak. I hate to see someone being picked on. I still remember how that felt, when I was just a little guy.

I have a hard time doing the Christian thing and turning the other cheek. It's probably that twenty percent redneck I have running through my veins.

I just never fully grasped the message. If you've already been slapped once, why would you tee it back up for them? I realize that the passage is metaphoric, but metaphors are used to help explain things. Like I said, it's very confusing. I must have missed that Sunday school class.

Frankly, it wouldn't bother me if the Almighty decided to give those cowardly bullies a couple of swift kicks, before He lets them in the Gate or maybe send them south for a weekend to get a taste of Hell.

I know I shouldn't go around feeling this way. Forgiving is the hardest thing for me to do. Especially, when they did it on purpose.

When I was a small child, Miz Lena told me, "Honey Baby, if yuh let hate stay in yore heart too long, it'll turn the good, in yuh, to bad. It happens when yore asleep. Before yuh know it, the Devil owns yore soul. If yuh feel like he's close by, just say, "Git thee behind me, Satan."

I already had a couple of night-time "hoolie-goolies" to deal with.

There was the half-frog-half-man creature with bugged-out eyeballs and frog legs under my bed. I'd never actually seen him, but that's what I imagined him to be. I'd take a run and jump. That way, he couldn't grab me by the ankles and pull me under.

Not just that, but every so often, a misty, blue-grey ghost woman stood over by the drapes and just stared at me. Her, I could see but just barely. She kinda looked like Mrs. Moody, from Bowling Green, Ky.

Mrs. Moody owned and ran a pre-school operation out of her home, just a few minutes up the hill. She had a big sign in her front yard that read, "Mrs. Moody's Happy Children Pre-School." When

Mom needed a break, Dad would drop us off at Mrs. Moody's for the day.

Pre-school makes her sound too legit. She didn't teach anything. She just turned on the TV. I can absolutely tell you that there were no "happy children" under her roof.

In actuality, Mrs. Moody was a mean old woman who wore dirty clothes and babysat ten or twelve kids, my two younger brothers and I included. All three of us were under the age of five. I was the oldest.

I remember her smelly house, her foul disposition, her awful body odor and her serving us small cartons of warm chocolate milk. She left it out rather than put it in the refrigerator. I registered complaints that fell on deaf adult ears.

Then, she'd order us to take a nap. I wasn't sleepy. That was a problem. I could just imagine what "real school" was gonna be like.

After a few days, watching what turns Dad took, I figured out how to get back home. As soon as Mrs. Moody looked the other way, I was gone. Dad drove me back. I kept escaping. Finally, Dad stopped taking us up there.

So, I'm already dealing with the frog-legged guy with crazy eyes, the Mrs. Moody ghost and now, I had to be on a nightly lookout for Satan attempting to penetrate my soul and suck the love from my heart.

At night, just after Grand Mom tucked me in and "cut off the lights", I lay there in the dark with great anxiety, trying to get rid of any hate that might be lingering in my heart.

No telling how many times I told the devil to get behind me. To this day, I still tell him to get gone. I guess it works. I'm still here.

Those of us who have been up and down a few times have found out who our true friends are.

I know folks who spend a lot of time running back-and-forth. If it appears you're down and out, they run to the "I told you so" side of the field. When you get up and over, they scurry back and say, "I knew you'd do it." Yeah. Right.

Here lately, my gut-voice has been after me to forgive those who have done me wrong. That's a tough one. If someone's sorry, truly sorry, I end up giving them another shot at it. Really, two chances are enough.

It's a good thing that I've been given second chances on stupid stuff I've done. A lot of it, in an inebriated state of being. I used to tell them that I never got drunk but that I'd been "over-served" many times.

You may remember Carol O'Conner. He was a fantastic actor and a good guy. He was best known for his Archie Bunker TV character. I made his acquaintance in the '80s.

He owned a great little restaurant, on Camden, in Beverly Hills, called Ginger Man. It had a hip bar crowd and served up some pretty good chow.

In the evenings, they had a "who's-who" clientele. I used to meet up with Peter Lawford, and we'd drink the night away. Peter was over-served every night.

At a certain hour of the evening and after several toss-backs of Jack Daniels, I put on my sunglasses and became Ray Charles. I pulled up a chair to complete strangers, looked to the ceiling, swayed back-and-forth and played their tables like a piano.

I sang, "Hit the Road, Jack" and "I Can't Stop Loving You." Often, they'd sing along with me. Sometimes, others joined in.

Everyone seemed to have a good time with it. Mr. O'Conner did not. I remember him telling me, "Bill, I'm going to forgive you, this one more time." He gave me a lot of second chances.

I finally stopped drinking, several years ago. I had to. I got into too much trouble, and I wasn't my best the following day. Plus, attorney's fees were eating me up.

So, my annual check list looks pretty good. I'm happy, but I could be happier. I'll work on that. I hope that my stories have been contributing. I'm close to done. It's taken me a while to adjust to a much slower pace of life, but I'm getting there. It's about time.

I'm sure that my wife, Jana, and I are where we should be. Returning to my Tennessee roots was just what the doctor ordered. A lot of very nice and decent people back here.

Most importantly, I've decided that I'm gonna give it all I have to forgive a few people. In fact, I have a couple of "I'm sorrys" that I hope will be accepted. Sometimes, all anybody needs is a second chance.

If you have a mind to, make yourself a list. Put some thought into what you can do to make yourself happier. Let go of the junk that, chances are, you've been carrying around for far too long.

If one of your New Year's resolutions has to do with dieting, remember that forgiving or being forgiven can take a load off.

Happy New Decade, Y'all.

THESE LAST FEW YEARS HAVE BEEN A TRIP

I'm getting to that age where I look everywhere for my keys and finally realize that they're in my hand.

Things that meant something to me no longer do. My materialistic side has given way to comfort. My ego is contained. My past, very decadent lifestyle has been replaced with a resurrected belief in the Almighty. Don't get me wrong. I'm not a born-again religious fanatic. Far from it. But I'm a better man than I was.

It was just a few short years ago, in the wee hours of the morning that I got on my knees, in the living room of our home in Malibu, California and asked for help from the Man Upstairs. It was the first time, in decades, that I'd poured my heart out to God.

Not since Vietnam had I asked the Almighty for anything. I guess you could say that I didn't feel like I deserved any sort of divine consideration. I'd pretty much crossed the line on every one of the "Thou shalt nots." I was fairly certain that I was gonna end up doing time in the hottest corner of Hell.

Family betrayal, lost loved ones, demons from the past and mere crumbs of friendships weighed heavily on my mind and tugged at my heart every waking morning. It got to be laborious just to drag myself out of bed.

My belief that if I made a mess of money I'd be happy turned out to be wrong. From the time I was a teenager, I was led to believe that the solve-all to everything was the almighty buck. It'll keep your electricity on, but it stops way short of real happiness.

Depression's an evil cloud that sits overhead and rains on you day and night. If there's no sunshine but, instead, just a little drizzle, you settle for that being a good day. But, sooner than later, here comes another storm.

Drugs mixed well with my morning coffee. My only outings were to the golf course or driving Jana to the grocery store. I stayed close to home with our dogs, stopped talking to people and basically shut down. Those closest to me had broken my heart. I didn't see it coming.

I faked it. Very few knew what I was going through. Frankly, the details were too embarrassing to talk about to anybody. That's not my style, anyway.

Writing this column has been the only time in my life that I've ever let my guard down or shared this much about myself to anyone. I believe that privacy and dignity go hand-in-hand.

Over the years, I've seen several shrinks. Psychology is fascinating to me. I know that it helps many people to get past their problems, but I'm of the opinion that, if you don't watch it, you come out of the sessions with discovery of more problems than you went in with.

Besides, there was no way that I was going to tell a stranger sitting in a chair, with their framed degree hanging on the wall, my innermost thoughts and secrets. If I had, chances are, they'd have refunded my money and wished me good luck.

I was so depressed that, more than once, I thought about ending it all. It was the least that I could do for my beautiful wife, Jana. She deserved so much better than I could give of myself. It gets really weird when you start thinking that taking your life is a "solve-all."

Jana's truly a wonderful human being. I'm very lucky to have her by my side. Twenty-four years, so far. She and I are like Velcro. Her heart is pure, and she loves me for me. That makes things easy, because, at this point in my life, I don't think I can make too many more changes.

All my life, I've been different. Different than my family. Different than most anyone. Seems like all the different kinds of people, from the corners of everywhere, end up in Los Angeles, working in the entertainment business. The lost get unlost. I was in the "rat race" for forty years. I had a good run.

The subject of God doesn't come up much in Los Angeles. Acknowledgement of the Almighty's existence kinda puts a damper on the lifestyle. Showbiz has a religion all its own. "Tis better to get than give."

Actually, that sounds more Shakespearian than holy. But, you get the point. There's a good chance that some of my friends, in Los Angeles, won't like this, but, deep down, they know it's true.

So, there I was in my living room, in front of the fireplace. For the first time in a long time, I was getting ready to ask the Almighty for some guidance.

I hadn't planned to get on bended knee, but there was a voice that came from within, telling me that if I was serious, that I needed to kneel. Down I went.

I didn't quite know where to start. There was a lot of ground to cover. I prayed for a while. It felt good. I hadn't had the feeling I was experiencing for quite some time. Like, decades.

Not more than 48 hours later, out of the blue, it came to me, that I should return to where I started. Where I felt my best. Where I had a fighting chance to find myself and reclaim my soul. We made some arrangements, and Jana, the dogs and I, were on our way to Tennessee.

It was the first time, since I was a kid, running with my dog, Prince, through the country fields of Middle Tennessee, that I'd taken a "leap of faith." I had my fingers crossed.

In the back of my mind, I reckoned that if I could hold on and live a little longer, I could do enough good to even out my wrongs, and I'd be put on the list at the Pearly Gates allowing me an unencumbered entry.

I wasn't sure what I was going to do, once we got back here. I thought maybe I'd try my hand at writing. The only stuff I'd written my entire adult life were sales presentations and commercials.

After all this time, maybe I'd get back into radio and do an air shift. That's where I started, when I was 14, working six-hour weekend shifts for my dad.

I figured I'd try to do something that truly contributed to others. Not for the money but for the derived pleasure of making people feel good. That may come off a little corny, but that's what I thought.

I ended up, here in Cleveland, where I lived with my two younger brothers and Dad back in the late 50s and the first two years of the 60s. The happiest years of my childhood. Cleveland's still a great little town.

We've been back here for over three years. Initially, we thought we'd be here for no more than six months. Enough time for me to see how this writing thing was gonna work out.

I've been writing for this paper for over 26 months. Over 100 stories. I had no idea that I had all this in me.

Way back when, to protect my heart, I stuffed away a lot of my childhood. There were just too many episodes of unhappiness and tragedy that I didn't want to think about. So, almost all of my childhood memories, good and bad, got locked up somewhere in my brain.

Somehow, I've managed to sift through it all, pluck out the good stuff and leave the rest in the ashes of my mind. I am no longer demon-infested. It's a really good feeling.

In a way, I have all of you to thank for the weight, that I've carried for most of my life, being lifted. Writing my little ditties for you has been my pleasure and provided me with some great therapy.

Your response to me has been overwhelming. I've received thousands of emails and Facebook messages from you. You're very kind.

I've also written two books of short stories about my Southern upbringing. If it hadn't been for my grandmother, Miz Lena and Elizabeth, Dimple,

Clarence, Ole Tom and so many other great Southerners I grew up around, there's no telling how I would have ended up.

This is my last column for a while. I have some other things I want to pursue before they turn out the lights.

My thanks to Alison Gerber and Lisa Dalton for the opportunity to share a little bit of me with you. They're nice people. Maybe, somewhere down the road, they'll let me drop in to say hello to you. Also, my thanks to the Tennessee Press Association for the awards. I'm humbled and honored.

And, last but not least, thank you, God. It's great to have you back in my life. I'm trying to be good. As you know, that's a full-time job.

So, there you go, folks. It's a wrap. I'm gonna miss you guys.

OLD BARNS AND SOUTHERN MEMORIES

Hey, Ya'll. It's been awhile. My wife, Jana, and I have just returned from a six-month visit to Southern California, from which we'd been gone for almost four years. It was good to see our furniture and clothes and Jana's shoes.

Nothing much has changed out there. There's just more of them. They're still running at tilt-speed and clamoring for that pot of gold. If they find it, they'll go buy some shiny things and hope that they're noticed.

The fires started up just as we were leaving. They'll last for a few months. Pretty much, right up to the mudslide season. Then, an earthquake or two. California, especially Southern California, has, unfortunately, passed its prime. Too many people. An almost nonexistent code of ethics.

It sure is good to be back home. I told a friend of mine, Johnny Holden, that I'm never leaving, again. Sometimes, no matter how smart or wise you think yourself to be, you hop over the fence and realize that the grass just isn't any greener. I'm home. Tennessee is where they'll plant me. Can I get an "Amen"?

I felt the first hint of Autumn the other day. A cool wind reminded me of days to come. It won't be long till cold heads our way. No more sitting outside at night. Gotta bring the dog in.

By the way, we got ourselves a new pup. We named him, Rebel. He's a black-tri Australian Shepherd. Just six months old. He's a handful.

In the 50s, when I was a little boy, growing up out in the countryside of Middle Tennessee, I remember standing on the hill, out back of Widow Thompson's farm. The cooled winds of Fall were blowing. I closed my eyes and pointed my face to the sun. As chilly as it was that day, my face warmed up.

My grandmother's housekeeper, Elizabeth, told me that the Almighty was reaching His arms out to me and warming my soul. She said that sort of stuff all the time. All that I could think about were "the long arms of God." Elizabeth told me to always be on the lookout for signs from Heaven.

There are countless clues to this life, that God throws out there for us every day. You have to be present, clear-headed and keep an eye out for them. Some are more obvious than others.

They're hardly noticeable, if at all, to the untrained eyes of a city slicker. I think you probably have to have been raised in the South. Even better, a little ways out in the country, past the last row of urban lights and asphalt covered streets.

Far enough out that the night sky is black and the sprays of a million stars are bright silver. The way the Almighty meant them to be seen. The way it was before the South started getting crowded.

Every year, in order to accommodate a growing population, they tear apart a few more farms and build, row-after-row, little, look-alike houses with postage-stamp-sized yards.

Off-the-road farms, tucked behind shade trees, where mothers and fathers raised their families and worked their lands, are, one-by-one, being parceled, plotted and paved to make way for ambitious developers' interpretations of structural progress.

When they're done, there's no sign of what was there. More of our history is completely erased. If you ask one of the old-timers for directions, they're liable to tell you to "go down the road a bit and turn left, where the Thompson's farm used to be."

Gone, for the most part, are those big, old, leaning, bleached-out grey barns, standing up close to the road. Built with little more than handsaws, hammers and 30 d nails pounded into creaking beams and poles. Patched-up and held together by generations of family pride and country muscle.

Back then, people built things to last. When it was their time to go and meet their Maker, Momma and Daddy handed down the farm to their children. The house, the land and the barn.

It's still that way with some. The farm stays in the family. They wouldn't sell it to you for a trillion dollars. There are some things in this life that just aren't for sale. God bless those folks.

Most every one of those old barns started out whitewashed or painted red. Whatever their original color had been is faint or just flat gone.

The rooftops were almost always heavy sheets of tin, eventually covered with strains of purplish-blue and mosaic-orange and crimson-rust caused by the elements and time. When Father Time teams up with Mother Nature, the worn results can be almost poetically beautiful. Especially old barns.

If I had to pick a painting of a new barn or an old one, I'd go for the old one. More character. Vintage is in a class all its own. In some ways, I can relate to those old barns. Especially the ones that lean a little.

I have stenciled memories of walking toward the barn on cold mornings. So cold, that you kept your hands in your pockets and when you talked, your words came out like small clouds.

Men, who'd gotten up and out the door before the roosters had a chance to announce another morning, stood congregated in front of and just inside the big, open double-doors of the barn. That's where they met every morning.

As I neared, I could hear murmurs of conversations, mixed with light laughter and morning coughs. Co-workers, black and white men, having one last smoke and another half-cup of coffee, before they stepped out and put their backs into another day.

I love those old barns, where mama hens and their chicks sought shelter from the storms and cold weather. Where tobacco was hung every summer's end. Where cows were milked and swallows and owls nested, hatched their babies and taught them to fly.

If you've ever stood in a barn, just as the summer sun's going down, it's a good bet that you've seen fleets of swallows darting in and out. They're like little blue jets! They come right at you, then, at the last second, cut perfectly around you.

Progress has gobbled up a whole bunch of farms. So, there are less-and-less barns and haylofts. A place where we used to swing way out on a thick, brown rope, let go and soft-land on open bales of golden hay. It's something you can do rain or shine.

Haylofts, where Billy got a little sugar from Suzy. Sometimes, the sugar was so good that Billy was inspired to carve a heart, with his and Suzy's initials in it, on one of those thick hardwood posts, holding up the barn.

Hay is one of my favorite smells of barnyard living. It ranks right up there with horse manes. One whiff of either and my mind races back to my Tennessee childhood and has me standing in front of a barn.

I still have pictures in my head of an old abandoned barn that sat atop a slope on my grandmother's farm. In the summer, I'd walk out to it and wonder how much longer it was gonna be before it fell over. It was still standing in the 80s.

When I was a kid, I went to a few parties that were held in barns. They just pushed everything to the back. Plenty of room.

Friends, neighbors, most of them first, second and third cousins, and a mess of in-laws, danced, twirled and clogged all night, to toe-tapping fiddles, banjoes and guitars plugged into small, buzzing amplifiers.

There was one old fellow, on the only microphone, hollering out nasal dance moves and directions of "Swing your partner" and "Do-si-do" to the appreciative, whooping, hooched-up and glistening steppers.

We kids ran in and out of the barn till some woman caught one of us by the arm and told us to "take it outside." Out we went. We chased cats and ran after each other, in between the trucks and cars that were parked up around the barn and across the front pasture.

I'm not sure that there's any other kind of structure, in America, that symbolizes unity more than barns. It took a lot of men, white men and black men, to build and raise those barns. Each one of them still standing is, in a way, a monument.

I've always tried to put myself in the other guy's shoes. I guess I understand why some of us take great offense to statues and monuments of Confederate soldiers and generals. I get it. But, many of those statues are part of our history, too. It's a touchy subject.

Why not erect a statue, memorializing a black leader, right next to the Confederate one, and we can all move on?

How about this? All barns, 50 years or older, should be declared state historical landmarks. All of us, white and black, should be able to agree on this idea. It's simple enough.

Somebody call Governor Lee. Let's save some of our mutual history while we can. Barns are reminders of our Southern roots. Built with determination and the cooperative strengths of black and white men.

No doubt, they got some help from the "long arms of God."

IT'S, REALLY, ALL ABOUT THE TRUTH

Firstly, I sure do appreciate all the emails I received from you in regard to me starting back up with this paper. I'm good for a column every two weeks, till the first of the year, and we'll go from there. Awfully nice of Lisa Denton to allow me some space to visit with you. I haven't been writing for the past several months, so I'm a little rusty.

My wife, Jana, and I just turned another year older. Jana's birthday was September 26th. Mine was October 2nd. We're just six days apart, if you don't count the other 19 years, 359 days. Jana has now officially been with me half of her life. I really love her.

If you knew what I know, about my life, you'd be just as shocked as am I, that I'm still here. And, in relatively good shape.

I've kept my Marine Corps weight of 190 pounds, but I don't stand a chance of ever fitting into my uniforms again. I'm still in there, I've just shifted a bit. Adios, 30" waist. It was nice knowing you.

Because I am my frugal grandmother, Miz Lena's, grandson, I've held on to several pairs of pants, with waist sizes 32" to 35". They're too small for me, but I have them neatly folded and stacked in a couple of wardrobe boxes, just in case. A mess of beautiful leather belts as well.

I'm pretty sure that the only exercise that I could ever do to get back to a 30" waist would be to go work in the salt mines. I'm back home where everything tastes better. Damn those East Tennessee "meat-and-threes."

I've thought of giving my slacks to Goodwill, but they're like brand new and were costly. I hate to get rid of "brand new." Still, I know, deep down, I'll probably never don them again. I may give it another year and if my waistline hasn't dropped down, they'll get passed on.

In the future, should you see a thin, homeless man sporting a pair of practically new, cuffed slacks, they're probably from me. The matching belt...that's me, too.

When I was a young buck, running the town, throwing back shots of Jack Daniels, driving fast cars and going crazy, "Father Time" was the last thing on my mind. I was too busy having the time of my life, as was evidenced by all those speeding tickets and the altercations I got myself into.

Had I, as Miz Lena used to tell me, just counted to 10 before reacting, I could have saved myself a lot of bruises, busted knuckles, stiff fines, eye-popping attorney's fees and valuable time. In all candor, there were inebriated nights where I couldn't remember my name, much less count to 10.

That was a rough patch of time. They say, "Live and learn." I guess God decided to let me learn some things the hard way. Er, Uh, thanks, Lord.

These days, I prefer to coast rather than speed to get anywhere. However many years that I have left on this green earth won't be in "rush mode." No sense in hurrying toward the finish line.

My rearview window is filled to the brim with memories good and bad. Mostly good.

I'm, pretty much, split down the middle. Half my thoughts are of the "here-and-now" and the other half are dedicated to "days gone by." That format has managed to keep me balanced. Sorta, kinda.

Some of my memories are monumental. The birth of my son; the day I met my wife, Jana; our dogs; my first and last day in Vietnam and the year that I gave up drugs and drinking. There's plenty more.

I try not to think of the bad stuff. I've already been through it all. So, there's no need to relive it. I refuse to waste any more waking days on past, unpleasant circumstances or undesirable characters. Looking back, I realize that I've thrown away so much God-given time.

Besides, there's plenty more negativity out there, these days, with which to contend. I sure hope that we, sooner than later, get on the same page and begin healing the tortured and cracked heart of our beloved USA. We used to be in it together, regardless of our politics. Times have changed.

Even though he was before my time, I've always loved the way Teddy Roosevelt described our American attitude about righteousness, "Speak softly and carry a big stick." That's what I grew up on. There are a few of us out there who could use a brush up course on the speaking softly thing.

No matter who's right or wrong, you gotta admit, these last few years have just about worn us out. I sure wish our leaders could find a conduit for peaceful and meaningful solutions to all the junk that's going on out there.

The Rotarian Four Way Test starts with, "Is it the truth?" Used to be, especially in the South, that a look in the eyes, a handshake and a man's word was all that was needed. Nowadays, we need attorneys to look over everything, before we commit to anything. Many times, the contract's not worth the paper on which it's written.

I used to wonder why the Almighty didn't hand down eleven Commandments. I've always thought that there's one missing, "Thou shalt not lie." Had God added that one, I guess we'd all stand a good chance of going to Hell.

I'm not sure if many of us know what the truth is anymore. Some of us lie so much that you end up believing the lie that sounds closest to the truth. I, for one, don't want to live the rest of my limited time on Earth dealing with chaos. Some people like it. I don't.

Sit and think for a minute. Would our parents or their parents, your grandparents, have allowed us to get to this level of dishonesty? I think not.

They'd make very sure that what we said and did was considerate of others and truthful. That was pretty much the creed of our great nation. Most especially, the South. Being honest was one of the top three priorities. The other two were our God and our country.

The United States of America, that I saddled up and flew halfway around the globe to defend is, sadly, way off course. No longer do we fight for prevailing truth and to do what's right. It's more about what can be gotten away with. Principals, for which we once stood, have given way to greed and conveniences. It's a dirty, rotten shame.

When I was very young, I asked my grandmother's housekeeper, Elizabeth, if she thought that I was crazy. She told me that the whole world was crazy and that, "Pretty soon, da Lord is gonna come down here and fix things." Elizabeth made that statement to me well over 65 years ago.

Lord, I know You're busy, but we sure would appreciate it if You could come down here and get us back on the right track. Please heal our country and this world. In my humble opinion, it's way past time, Lord.

P.S. God, Thanks for all the time you've given me down here. And, thanks for all the stuff. And, thanks for making me an American.

WHEN DID IT ALL BECOME SO POLITICAL?

I know some people who would rather talk politics than eat. Me, I'd rather eat. I don't think we've ever been so political as nowadays. Say something that's not so complimentary about a Republican, and you're liable to get shot.

Same goes for bad-mouthing passive-aggressive Democrats. Except, rather than shoot you, they'll just slap you to death.

It's all begun to be a bit much. Grown-up men and women hollering at each other about their differences of opinion. What they should be doing is figuring out what to do in case of a tail-spin. If we don't watch it, we're not far from taking an unwanted nose-dive.

Frankly, I couldn't care less which party is in office. Say whatever you like, but they're both pretty much the same. For every bad thing you can come up with about a Democrat, there's something that's just as bad about a Republican.

I truly believe that, next to race, politics is what has caused everybody to separate ranks. It's crazy how we treat one another based on our political party affiliations.

When I was growing up, over in Middle Tennessee, back in the 50s, people kept how much money they had and who they voted for to themselves. Obviously, that Southern tradition is long gone.

Dad was in radio. He felt, rightfully so, that radio personalities were better off keeping their personal politics to themselves. It just wasn't good business to spout off about a politician. No matter what, you were bound to offend someone. Worse yet, that "someone" might be an advertising client. That's a very understandable explanation.

With my grandmother, Miz Lena, it was less psychological and much more to the point. Ask her why she didn't discuss who she voted for, and she'd tell you, right quick, "Cause it ain't nobody's bizness. That's why." Also, easy to understand.

There are 8000 UFO sightings every year. Not one of them has landed. It's no wonder. If they're observing the way we talk to and treat each other and watching the news and debates on Fox, CNN, MSNBC, and the rest of them, they've gotta be scratching their over-sized, Preying Mantis heads.

I guess they figure there's no need to bother communicating with us. It must seem inevitable to them that sooner or later, the Universe keeper will get fed up with the way we're treating our planet and one another and mash down on the "blow-up" button.

Why would they want to be friends with a society of humanoids who seem to be bent on destroying most of what God created for them?

The Rain Forest is going up in smoke. Our streams and oceans and seas are in trouble. Drugs are more rampant than ever and our crime rates go up every year. But, oh yes, the stock market's up. That oughta take care of everything.

Every time you turn around, there's some country, that I don't care anything about visiting, making nuclear threats at us. Another thing, there are some pretty weird people running some of those countries. Of course, they could say the same thing about us.

There's a part of me that would just as soon get whatever fighting we need to do out in the open and over with. There's no sense wasting time meeting them in the parking lot, if all we're gonna do is yell at each other.

Sorry if this offends any of you Flower Children. I just think that things are gonna continue down the path we're heading and one of these days, we'll find ourselves in a bad situation. You never think that it's too late till it's too late.

I get the philosophy of "make love not war." But, there's a bunch of them, over there, who, unfortunately, better understand muscle and our willingness to fight it out, if they step on our principals or tread on our beliefs. It's important for us to be united in this regard.

My America is not weak. We're plenty empathetic and compassionate, but we stand our ground and don't allow the line to be crossed. That's what makes us who we are. We're not going to achieve peaceful solutions by shooting basketball with Kim Jong Un or having a "love-in" with Putin.

It's important for them to know that we can't be played, and that we bow to no one.

It may be that some of you find my opinion a touch aggressive. I guarantee you that anyone who has actually traveled to a foreign land and engaged in combat understands, full well, what I'm saying is true.

We can contain them, without physical confrontation, by standing strong. Think about it, you don't hear about any country out there threatening Russia. I disagree with Russia's policies, but you gotta respect their hard-line toughness.

I understand people wanting to get across the border and start new lives for their families in the good ole US of A. Why wouldn't they? America's the greatest country in the world. Most everyone would like to have a piece of America. I can't blame them. Still, it needs to be done the right way. It's our country, so it's our rules.

You never hear about Americans trying to sneak into Mexico or Yugoslavia or any other country, for that matter. If we did happen to leave the States, I seriously doubt that another country would allow us to march down their streets in protest, carrying signs and screaming demands of them.

There's no grass greener than what we have on our side of the fence. What we take for granted is longed for and coveted by the rest of the world. I'm proud of that.

Hats off to our founding fathers and all those who have been or are in precarious parts of the world, heads high, and taking on the bad guys. If you think about it, we've been engaged in wars for some time, now. There's gotta be a better way.

Grand Mom was "old school" Southern and dipped in patriotism. She pulled over to the side of the road and insisted that we put our hands over our hearts as a funeral procession passed by. She wasn't much on singing but always joined in and belted out "God Bless America" anytime it played.

She constantly reminded me that we were special because we were Americans. Furthermore, she was positive that God had a special place in his heart for

Tennesseans. I believed her then, and I believe it now. We're blessed. I'd like it to stay that way.

In my humble opinion, it's time for us and the rest of the world to find ways to coexist in peace and harmony. I'm not sure that's possible, but it's worth the fight.

We've done all this and are still doing it to ourselves. Shame on us for allowing things to get to this point. There's an answer to it all. Stop doing it.

THIS YEAR, 2020, CAN KISS IT WHERE THE SUN DON'T SHINE

I trust that you had as good a Christmas as can be expected under our present circumstance. These times are trying, to say the least.

I don't know about you, but I'll be glad when this year is over. Hopefully, in this coming new year, we can get back to some normalcy. That is, after we've conquered COVID and gotten the ringing out of our ears.

We, as a country, have a whole bunch of healing to do. And, we're gonna have to do it on the run. There's no time to dilly-dally. My hope is that the time we've wasted snarling will be replaced with compassion and respect for one another. It may sound a little sappy, but that's the way I feel.

Maybe, we'll actually go back to being true fellow Americans. We need to assign a crew, comprised of a few from each side of the political aisle, to go up there and mop up that line that, in recent years, has severally divided us. While we're at it, let's get our standards and principals back up and running.

This year has been one like no other that I can remember. Just a few more days, and we'll be at the finish line. Step over it, and we're right back on next year's start line. Ain't it funny how life races on?

Chances are, someone in your family or a friend of yours has succumbed to this wretched Corona Virus. Thank God Almighty that no one in my family has caught it. However, I've lost several friends to it, including good ole Charlie Pride. As hugely successful as was he, he was humble and modest.

Back in the 70s, I booked Charlie in Northern California. He flew in early enough that we had time to get in a round of golf before that evening's concert.

We were both long hitters. I out drove him, but he played his irons much better than I.

I'll never forget him pulling out a sand wedge and hitting his ball straight up and over a huge cypress tree and landing on the green, a foot from the pin. He just smiled. I love those kinds of guys. We're gonna miss you, Charlie.

I've never really done well with New Year's resolutions. I don't remember how long ago I stopped making them. I'm not sure what they were. For years, they mostly had to do with me stopping drinking.

I usually made that resolution in the wee hours of the first day of January, after I'd drunk myself under the table. I mixed some religion with it. It went like this, "Please, God, I know that we've been down this road before, but if you can make all this go away, I'll be good from here on in."

Don't let anybody fool you. It's tough to stop drinking. When you're all alone and three-sheets-to-the-wind, you end up talking to God. No telling how many drunks the Lord has to listen to on any given night. Especially on New Year's Eve.

I can't say that the Almighty ever answered me right back. I don't guess, deep down inside, I thought He would. That was going a bit far for me to have expected Him to stop what He was doing and cure my drunken dizziness.

Hopefully, you won't find yourself in that predicament, come this New Year's Day. If you do, I've found that while you're suffering and waiting for some Divine Intervention, a couple of Bloody Mary's, heavy on the Worcestershire, and sunglasses can help.

When I finally quit drinking, all my puffiness went away. I began to think more clearly, and I dropped a few pounds. Now, I'm in my 70s. Weight is trying to pile on. I won't let it. Eating fruit and balanced meals is helpful. My wife, Jana, does what she can to make sure I'm getting the proper nutrients.

Ever notice that all the things that are good for you don't taste so good? What kind of man wants to eat yogurt, prunes and chew on a fruit bar, when you have Coca Colas in the fridge and Ritz crackers and peanut butter in the cupboard?

I know that I need to watch my diet. I'm not getting fat, but my cholesterol level is probably up. I say "probably", because I very seldomly go to the doctor. I don't do well with waiting and smells of sterility. Plus, their selection of magazines is downright boring. To whomever's in charge of office subscriptions, two words: *Sports Illustrated.*

There're all kinds of stuff I need to lay off of, but I just can't help it. It's the way I grew up. If I could, I'd stop eating biscuits and pepper gravy. But, I just can't. Besides, it's almost un-American.

I can say, for sure, if it weren't for pulled-pork barbeque sandwiches, pork chops, spare ribs, sausage and bacon, I definitely wouldn't eat pork.

Same goes for fried meats. Answer me this, how's a guy supposed to go through life without hamburgers? It's just not right. Same goes for french-fries. I guess you could say that they're my "forbidden fruit."

It took a while for the Devil to transform into a snake and then talk Adam into eating that apple. My bet is that if fried chicken had been the temptation, Adam would have folded right away. I assume that God must have invented chickens a little later on.

It sure would be great if we could go to bed, on December 31st, and awaken to a brand new year, filled with love and respect for one another. A new year of understanding and bipartisan participation in getting to the bottom of and curing the things that have become terribly obstructive to us all.

This upcoming New Year could turn out to be a good one, if we can find a way to bury the hatchet. Life's short. None of us have, comparatively speaking, that long to go before we ascend to our Maker.

We must find a way to get back to being who we were meant to be, before we got to here. We must be in it together.

I'm sure hoping that, when I expire, I head North rather than South. If not, I'm sure that I'll see several familiar faces down there. There's a good chance that I'd bump into my cousin, Ronny. He was a scoundrel.

He and that lying "so-and-so", who did me wrong last year, will probably be stuck waiting tables for eternity. More than likely, they'll be serving yogurt, prunes and fruit bars.

Have a Happy New Year, Ya'll. And, a belated Happy Birthday to Mrs. Margaret Varnell.

HOLLYWOOD DRINKIN' DAYS AND LASH LARUE

When I was a child, my grandmother, Miz Lena, told me, "Honey Baby, life by the inch is a cinch. Life by the yard is hard." Wish I'd listened to her. I could have saved myself some misery. Up until a while ago, I "broad-jumped" my way through most of my adult years.

I'd already had a good run in radio and TV. I was ready to make my mark in the entertainment business. I headed for "La La Land." Bright lights, big city. Hollywood where everything glitters.

It was the late 70s when I finally landed in Los Angeles. I got a job with Marty Ingles. He was married to Shirley Jones, at the time. She was a sweet lady. Marty was a failed "standup comedian" who'd had just one TV show, "I'm Dickens, He's Fenster." It starred Marty and John Astin. They only lasted a season.

Nobody could figure out why Shirley was with Marty. He was on the "top-ten list" of the most despised men in Hollywood. Up toward the top. Be that as it was, Marty showed me the ropes, and, shazam! Just like that, I became a celebrity broker. Turned out, I was a natural.

The whole job was talking celebrities into endorsing companies and products. Rather than go through their agents, we called the celebrities direct. Some of them were worried about what kind of public image, them doing commercials, would portray. They thought it might make them look like they were out of money or needed work.

When I got around to telling them the monetary offering, most of them stopped in their tracks, and I became their best friend for the moment. Their agents still got their 10% cut.

I enjoyed working with so many different famous and gifted men and women. It was really quite something for a country boy, like myself, to have the privilege of lunching with Elizabeth Taylor and her hair stylist, Jose Eber or chatting it up, over cocktails, with Orson Welles or Robert Wagner.

I played singles tennis over at the Beverly Hills Hotel, with Gene Wilder, Doug McClure, or Edd Byrnes. Edd was a great guy. You might remember him as the character, Kookie, on the TV series, "Seventy-Seven Sunset Strip."

Every once in a while, I played doubles with Ed Ames, Charlton Heston and the original Buck Rogers, Kem Dibbs, for $100.00 a set, at some rich guy's house, just below Kenny Rogers' Beverly Hills estate. They were all much older than I, so I ran them all over the court. I kinda felt guilty taking their money.

After my divorce from my son's mother, I dated actresses, almost exclusively. Some of them well known and several of them just getting started. Crazy on steroids.

There was almost always a function or a party going on. Mostly at the Beverly Hills Hotel, Merv Griffin's Hilton, the Beverly Wilshire Hotel or at someone's home.

My first A-list, Hollywood party was an "after-party" at Bob Hope's home, in Toluca Lake, just behind Universal and Warner Bros Studios.

Everybody, who was anybody, was there. Earlier that evening, Mr. Hope had performed to a sell-out crowd at the Universal Ampitheater.

Mr. Hope's home was beautiful. Old Hollywood. Walled and gated. Huge. Two swimming pools. Several guesthouses. The old stables were converted to a garage for his luxury car collection. Larger-than-life topiary hedge figures of horses, an elephant and a giraffe bordered his very own Par 3 golf course, out in his expansive backyard. All his housekeepers were Japanese and dressed in kimonos.

I remember reflecting on just how differently lives are lived. I thought of the black housekeepers who worked for my grandmother and practically raised me, Elizabeth and Dimple. I sure loved them. No telling what they would have thought.

My favorite actors were and are the old cowboys. Growing up, all us kids loved the Saturday morning cowboy TV shows. Hands down, my favorite was Lash Larue.

His calling card was a black bullwhip. He dressed in black, rode a black horse, named Black Diamond and holstered two pearl-handled pistols. Although he usually subdued the bad guys with his fists and that whip, if he was forced to, he'd shoot the gun out of their hand. Nobody ever died.

There's a famous Old Hollywood "watering hole" called Musso and Frank's. I used to like to stop in, in the late afternoon and down a couple. I was sitting at the long bar. Couldn't have been more than a dozen people in the place.

In walks a white-bearded, dapperly dressed guy, not so tall and in his 60s. I was probably 30. Even though there were plenty of empty bar stools, he sits down, right next to me. I ended up buying him a drink. He reciprocated and so on. We got pretty lathered up. He told me that his name was Al.

I told him my stories and he told me his. How he grew up in tough little towns in Louisiana, worked for the circus for a while, then moved to Los Angeles to pursue acting. I didn't recognize him, so I figured, just like so many other dreamers, he hadn't made it.

It wasn't until we were "three sheets to the wind" that he revealed to me that he was the one and only, Lash Larue. I was thrilled to meet him. I asked him a million questions, and he was only too happy to answer them.

Three young stocky guys were sitting at a table, just behind us. They were loud. Two or three times, one of them picked up their drinks at the bar and bump into me. I finally said something to one of them. He put his hands on me, and it was on.

This idiot threw a punch at me, missed, and I popped him a good one. He stepped back, holding his mouth and didn't act like he was gonna do anything. All of a sudden, just like in the movies, Lash was off his barstool, fists up and hollered out, "How many of you are there?"

Here came the other two. Lash hit one of them five times, before the guy knew what happened. I smacked the other one. Somehow, with all the hoopla, we switched opponents and kept on punching them, till the two of them were laid out. The third guy fast-stepped out the back door.

The bartenders helped the other two to their feet and told them to, "Get out and never come back." Lash and I sat back down and finished our drinks. What a way to meet an idol.

Lash and I met up several more times. Then, like it is in "Tinsel Town", we went our separate ways.

I heard he got religion and actually did some preaching but never stopped drinking. I can't say that it surprised me. During our drinking sessions, we talked some about God. Both of us were believers.

I remember telling Lash that I felt guilty drinking booze and talking about God, in a bar. He reminded me that all those Christians, back then, drank wine "till the cows came home." He told me, "If it wasn't for us drunks, God wouldn't have much to do." He'd lift his glass in toast and say, "To the Last Supper."

Lash Larue was my favorite cowboy, and he was quite a guy.

Through the grace of God, and support from my wife, Jana, I stopped drinking and brawling years ago.

I assume the Almighty has had a lot more time for others.

If you have a drinking problem, please get some help.

Scout Stamps

THE LAST NIGHT

March 16, 2021

Tonight will mark the last night Bill's terrestrial form.

A few days ago, Bill was really missing our pup, Scout. Somehow, during our talk, the story came up about him being wounded in Vietnam and in a state of delirium from malaria. His body temperature rocketed so high, the nurses at the hospital had to dump buckets of ice on his body.

During this altered state of delirium, Bill remembers turning into a waterfall that flowed through him.

I had heard the story a handful of times over the course of our 26 years together. The difference this time was that I said "Do you remember where the waterfall was?" My first thought was, Hawaii. Instead, he told me *The Smoky Mountains*.

It's my belief that tomorrow my baby will turn back into waterfall.

I humbly ask that you join me in prayer, one last time, for the safe passage of my baby's earthly form into the abyss of the Eternal Flame. I know his soul already resides in the loving arms of our Heavenly Father.

In Jesus' name, I pray.

Amen

~Jana

ADDENDUM:

March 17, 2021 @ 1p.m.
Time of Cremation

The skies were dark, then rumbled as the rain came down hard from 1pm-1:30pm, then stopped. It started raining again @ 4pm and poured through the night. I figure, it took my baby 1/2 to dissolve into ash and 2 1/2 hours to ascend to Heaven. The overnight rainpour is my sign my Beloved landed Home safely and is at peace.

The final transmutation from earth to fire into water.

It's sacred.

BILL'S LAST STORY

Bill left us with one more special parting gift. His last story: *Thinking About Living Some More.*

Lisa Denton, editor @ *Chattanooga Times Free Press*, and I put the finishing touches for its publication, Sunday, March 25, 2021.

Who knew this story would be so foretelling of Bill's impending passing? One really never knows how much time any of us have left.

Half of me seems to have died with him that fateful night. The world, once technicolor, has dimmed to black and white

At the end of Bill's story, I've included some lyrics to a song he was excited about. His words made me cry, so he decided to erase them. I reconstructed them from memory.

In contemplating the impact of Bill's stories, I've come to realize that what he accomplished most, was to make us feel, again, deeply.

Thank you for sharing your Sundays with us for all these years. We are tremendously grateful for your loyalty and great support.

Until we speak again.   ~Jana

THINKING ABOUT LIVING SOME MORE

You know what's great about life? Everything. From time-to-time, it may not seem like it. But, regardless of your sufferings, it's much better to be alive. Ask a dying man what he'd like the most, and he'll tell you, "more life." Another year or two, another month, another day. Just more life.

I've held dying men in my arms, over in Vietnam, and seen them suck in their last breath of mortal air, before they left Earth to be with their Maker. Watching life fade away leaves an indelible and unforgettable impression. A hole in your heart that never heals. One minute, they're with you and the next minute they're gone.

I know several people who have experienced near-death experiences, myself included. It's true that your whole life flashes before you. If you make it through something clicks inside. The little things in life mean more. You appreciate breathing.

I'm just past 72. That makes me an official senior citizen. According to those who keep track of these sorts of things, I've been one for a while. Hard to believe that I'm still here.

I never planned on living this long. I don't think anybody who knew me, back in the day, thought so either. First time in my life that I've had some spare time on my hands. I keep looking around for things to do. Old habits die hard.

At this point, there's not much wrong with me. Not sure if it has to do with my genes or, as my grandmother, Miz Lena, used to say, "a strong constitution." My only living blood brother and I have no way of tracking some of our family's medical history.

My father's mother died from complications giving him life. Dad's father skipped town and left him with his grandparents, on the Stamps' side of the family. What I do know is that most of the Stamps family live well into their 80s.

It's pretty much a slam dunk that they're all up there, basking on the beaches of Eternity. They were all good Christians. I'm afraid I can't say the same. You might say that my halo's a little rusty.

I've had invitations from fine folks to come to their church services. I fear for their safety. I'm pretty sure, the minute I entered their house of worship, the walls would tremble and fall. I'm hoping that my last years left will make up for some of my naughty past years. We'll see.

Other than an occasional aspirin, I don't take any prescribed medicine. I've maintained my weight and rarely go to the doctor. I'm fortunate that way.

So many of my fellow senior-citizen friends and associates have had heart attacks, strokes, knee and hip replacements, mental issues or have passed on. I'm pretty sure that I qualify for the mental issues' category. On some level, these days, I think we all do. It's kinda crazy out there.

I still wake up every morning thanking God for another glorious day. I learned to do that from a childhood acquaintance, Mr. Jenkins, an old war hero. If it weren't for my wife, Jana, I probably would have found a way to slide on outta here. I've had some dark years.

I've told Jana not to waste money on a tombstone and burying me on a hill in a cemetery with others that have passed on before me. Doubtful that I'll know any of them.

Just turn me back to ashes and set me up on the fireplace mantle, alongside our dogs, Cowboy, Scout, Chief and Tango. No funeral. No Celebration of Life, either. No sense in spending Jana's time or anyone else's, for that matter, mourning my passing.

Besides, I suppose I have enough ego in me, that I'd be terribly embarrassed if there was a poor turnout. Note to self, try not to die on Super Bowl Weekend.

So, here I be. Apparently, with more life left. I'm thinking, maybe I'll work on some self-improvement projects. I've given thought to trying to learn another language. Spanish or French. Seems like Spanish would be the easiest. I already know enough to ask for a cup of coffee or ask for the time.

Jana grew up in Switzerland, in a village halfway between Lausanne and Geneva. Out of necessity, she learned French, German and Italian. Those countries border Switzerland. Counting English, she speaks four languages. Right now, I speak two. West Coast and Southern.

I started writing a little over four years ago. It's been something to do. Looks like I'll probably write about something or another for the rest of my days. It's rewarding to hear from so many people and that you're enjoying my stories. Still, I feel like I can do more.

Like I said, I'm trying to stay on the good side of the Almighty. To be a contributor. To spread good cheer. I figure that if, on my last day, I'm involved in doing good stuff, as opposed to shooting somebody, that should make a good impression with God's Admissions Committee. At this point, every good deed counts.

If I do make it to the clouds of Heaven, there's always a chance that I'll be stopped at the Gates and told to report to Saint Peter's office . . . for a private, one-on-one testing session. Kind of a precursor. If so, I'm hoping it'll be an oral exam. I'm better that way than taking written tests. Multiple-choice-question tests can be confusing to me.

Kinda like the DMV written test. It usually takes me more than one try to pass, even though I can drive just fine. I know about the right time to turn on my blinker but not the exact number of feet required by law. If Saint Pete will give me a chance to explain some things, I think I have a fighting chance.

FEELS LIKE

Feels like I'm dying. Like it's the end of the road.

I have more life. But not for much more.

Tired of carrying the load.

All that keeps me going is your loving ways,

Your tender touch and those sweet lips.

Feels like I'm going to miss you when I'm gone.

GOOD GRIEF

By Wanda Mayfield

Heart is broken

Spirit weeps

The silence is deafening.

Time isn't healing wounds of the soul.

Memories are fading.

One breath at a time with faith seeking strength.

Reality is sharp.

People love when you're happy. They fear your

sadness and withdraw.

Things you shouldn't do, but you will:

Second guess yesterdays. All the why's, what if's, I should haves won't change anything.

Instead: Be one with your soul.

Trust our Creator for guidance.

Test your wings when you're ready, Ride a current of courage, Look ahead, not back.

Believe ⚘ Breathe ♥ And Fly 🦋

FINAL THOUGHTS

All Bill ever wanted was some peace and to be loved by his father and son. He never could find peace. Love was, at best, elusive.

I'm certain he knew he was loved by me, unconditionally.

I've witnessed too much suffering to pretend like it doesn't exist. Once you start serving others through Christ, you realize it's all around. No need to go to Africa to be cognizant of it. Children, animals, old folks. They're everywhere and they are alone. No one to protect them. Everyone silent. Detached. Traumatized by the magnitude of what our world has become.

Constant physical noise. Trucks, sirens, helicopters, blowers, TV, loud and obnoxious neighbors and their barking dogs. The list goes on. Bill's the one who made me aware of the loudness of our world. Hard to think straight and balance your soul in this constant state of confusion. That's a sure sign we're being manipulated.

It wasn't just that kind of noise that tested Bill's sanity daily, but the chaos in our heads and the hole in our hearts. The never-ending hurt caused by those closest to us. He was different and special. Easily labeled the "black sheep."

Jealousy, bickering and constant gossip from both our families deepened the wounds. Bill was outspoken and told it like it was. They didn't like that much. But behind his brutal honesty, he was loyal to the core.

While the privileged were going to the pizza parlor and taking girls out on dates, Bill was at war. Didn't he deserve a little respect, some space and understanding when he came back? Instead, they treated him like there was something wrong with him. Of course, there was something wrong. How could there not be? He literally had just walked through Hell and back. Fighting for his country. What did they do, except serve themselves?

Bill's greatest gift after leaving Vietnam was a prostitute. Her name was Kim, from Kim Village in Okinawa. She nursed him back to life. I'm grateful to her. She helped him forget what he'd just gone through, even if it was for just a little while. Bill gave her a refrigerator. The nicest present she'd ever received. He understood, all too well, the underdogs of this world. He was one, himself.

Throughout the years, Bill did so much for all those whom he loved. But, he never gave more than he did to his son. Only to see it turn on him.

Truth like justice is seldomly pretty to face. Rather brutal, slicing and final. Can't move forward with clarity without analyzing the facts and laying down the sentence.

I believe Judgement day is upon us all. All in God's timing.

Who says biblical times ended 2,000 years ago? We each play a part in the story. At the end of the day, who are you? What did you stand for? How did you help your fellow human being? Or, not.

Everything any of us have said or done, or not done or not said, is recorded. There is no escaping your lower self, unscathed, without a "Come-to-Jesus-Moment." That point in your life when you realize the depth of the sins you've committed. All the big and small ones that you've managed to burry and rationalize away.

There are plenty of spiritual individuals, out there, who think they're good people. That they're just fine with God. I was one of them. That will not save you.

It is only when you repent candidly and sincerely. When you comprehend the meaning, both literally and symbolically, of the sacrifice of the Blood of Jesus Christ and plead "Please forgive me", Redemption becomes available to you. Tabula Raza.

This cellular understanding of faith and soul requires a certain kind of intelligence. It's abstract.

I found it interesting to learn that Einstein had a hard time thinking multi-dimentionally. That's where faith fills in the gap.

A concept I heard some time back has proven helpful to me. Think of the brain as a computer. It's nothing unless you plug it in. What it connects to is electricity. It's invisible. Strangely enough we have no problem believing in that miracle.

Christian faith requires sincerity and commitment. Many will find God for a moment or a day, maybe longer. The discipline proves too difficult to sustain for most. It's a conscious choice to be faithful, truthful and kind. No need to be perfect. Little lies big lies, they're all the same after a while.

It's like a cancer that eats away the good of our collective soul.

In my world there is no more room for the toxic person. The actor. The one who fools you, over and over again, just because you want to keep loving them. They look good, they sound good, but that's as far as it goes until they go back to their corrupt self.

As Bill would sometimes say "We're all full up with crazy, here."

I believe God is good and everywhere, all the time. Vibrational energy.

But, the Devil also resides in the fiber of the macro and the micro.

The world lacks depth. It's become too loud. Full of meaningless banter. I refuse to ignore the abuse, suffering, absurdity and injustice that is present and for all to see. And, pretend everything is alright.

Most people are in shock these days. Probably without realizing the full extent of their mental apathy. Empathy is hard to live by. There are so many things that are wrong with this chapter in our collective lives. And yet somehow, we're being led to believe that this is "acceptable."

How do we wrap our arms and head around it all? It's overwhelming and easily watered down, when some say "Well, that's just the way the world is." I think not. We are better than that. We were not created by a Supreme Intelligence to end up accepting the unacceptable.

Children sex-trafficked. Boys and girls raped before they get a chance to reach puberty. Sometimes within their own family. This would have to be the one sin God could not possibly forgive. Why these pedophiles don't get the electric chair is beyond me. If stealing the soul and spirit of children isn't the worst of crimes, then what is?

I equally mourn the estimated 6 million horses that I read died in World War I and all those taken to conquer the West that perished along the way, piled on top of each other along the passes. Unspoken massacres. In present history, my heart sobs over all the animals currently in cages and used for experimentation. It's shameful and barbaric. Do you have any idea just how tough a horse really is? It takes the unthinkable to kill a healthy one.

Aside from those atrocities that linger on the back-burner of our minds, we are constantly bombarded with dreadful reporting, non sensical and violent movies and, overly excitable, out-of-touch commercials.

We're all slowly going mad and losing our connection to Source in the abyss of encroaching darkness. None of us can truly be happy knowing all that we know. We don't have the luxury, anymore, to pretend like we're ignorant.

As I see it, the genesis of our current situation is not about politics, religion, color of skin or gender. It boils down to who the individual really is. Not who they want to be or pretend to be.

There are plenty of fake believers and narcissists out there, who think they are really good people. But, display lack critical thinking and basic human decency. Just as long as it serves their purpose, anything can be rationalized away.

Men and women with big egos and hardened hearts do not only reside in the metropolis. Small towns have their fair share of hicks trying to be somebody, too.

The bully will always exist. That title is not necessarily reserved for the one who physically pushes people around. It can equally come from someone manipulating your emotions, testing your sanity and taking advantage of your love for them.

As a child, adolescent and adult, I witnessed someone very close to me being treated with far less respect than she deserved. At the time, I wasn't strong enough to defend her. It was all very murky. Difficult family psychology to untangle.

Don't let others be mistreated in your presence. Take a stance. Grow a spine. Do what's right. I wish I had done so sooner.

I refuse to fold to the ordinary. To be complacent, trampled on. And then be expected to go about life like nothing's wrong. Forced to swallow one more tall man's manipulative schemes. Skilled professional liars. Black and white alike. All the while grieving my husband, an American hero.

"She'll get over it. She's too silly to know the difference. What's she going to do about it anyway?"

I've absorbed Bill in me. I'm now taking him out to the country.

He has given me clairvoyance and strength to see through the delusions and fallacies of this world.

Saved the only oxygen that was left, for me to live on. And, gave me the precious gift of discernment to speak Truth.

The least Bill deserves is to finally rest in peace, with dignity, in the bosom of Mother Nature. The great mother who is abundant in creation and loves us all. Especially, him.

If ever there were a Child of God. He was it.

I will wait for God to speak to me.

~Jana

SPECIAL THANK YOU

I'll be forever grateful to Dr. C.K. Phillips for shepherding me through the formatting of this book and his patient and steady demeanor.

CONTACT INFO

For any comments and feedback, please contact me:

Jana Stamps

jana310@aol.com

****

A creation of

Do & Well Productions

www.dowellproductions.com

Made in the USA
Columbia, SC
11 November 2021